Demystifying Machine Learning: A Statistical Modeling Guide for Everyone

Lars Hansen

TABLE OF CONTENTS

Chapter 1: Introduction to Machine Learning

Understanding Machine Learning

Machine learning has become a buzzword in today's technological landscape, and it is crucial for everyone, regardless of their background, to have a basic understanding of this concept. This subchapter aims to demystify machine learning and provide a comprehensive overview of its principles and applications. Whether you are a statistician, data scientist, or simply someone interested in statistical modeling, this content will equip you with the knowledge needed to comprehend and appreciate the power of machine learning.

Machine learning is a branch of artificial intelligence that focuses on developing algorithms and statistical models that enable computers to learn from data and make predictions or decisions without being explicitly programmed. It involves the use of statistical techniques to analyze large datasets, identify patterns, and develop models that can generalize and make accurate predictions on new, unseen data.

In this subchapter, we will delve into the fundamental concepts of machine learning, starting with the different types of learning algorithms. We will explore supervised learning, where models learn from labeled data to make predictions, and unsupervised learning, where models identify patterns and relationships in unlabeled data. We will also discuss semi-supervised learning and reinforcement learning, two other important branches of machine learning.

Furthermore, we will explore the key steps involved in the machine learning process, including data preprocessing, feature selection, model training, evaluation, and deployment. We will emphasize the importance of data quality and the impact it has on the performance and reliability of machine learning models. Additionally, we will touch upon model evaluation metrics and techniques to prevent overfitting or underfitting.

Throughout this subchapter, we will showcase real-world examples and applications of machine learning, ranging from image and speech recognition to recommendation systems and fraud detection. By understanding these practical applications, you will gain insights into how machine learning can revolutionize various industries and improve decision-making processes.

In conclusion, this subchapter on understanding machine learning aims to provide a comprehensive introduction to the principles, types, and applications of this powerful field. Whether you are a statistical modeling enthusiast or simply curious about the world of machine learning, this content will demystify the concepts and arm you with the knowledge needed to appreciate the potential and impact of this rapidly evolving field.

Types of Machine Learning Algorithms

Machine learning is a powerful field that combines statistical modeling and data analysis to enable computers to learn from data and make intelligent predictions or decisions. There are several types of machine learning algorithms, each with its own unique approach and application. In this subchapter, we will explore some of the most common types of machine learning algorithms used in statistical modeling.

1.   Supervised   Learning   Algorithms: Supervised learning algorithms are trained on labeled data, where the input data is paired with corresponding output labels. These algorithms learn from this labeled data to predict the output labels for new, unseen data. Examples of supervised learning algorithms include linear regression, logistic regression, decision trees, random forests, and support vector machines. They are widely used for tasks such as classification and regression.

2.   Unsupervised   Learning   Algorithms: Unlike supervised learning, unsupervised learning algorithms are trained on unlabeled data, where there are no predefined output labels. These algorithms aim to find patterns or relationships within the data without any specific guidance. Clustering algorithms, such as k-means and hierarchical clustering, and dimensionality reduction techniques, such as principal component analysis (PCA) and singular value decomposition (SVD), are some examples of unsupervised learning algorithms.

3. Semi-supervised Learning Algorithms: Semi-supervised learning algorithms are a combination of supervised and unsupervised learning approaches. They are used when only a small portion of the data is labeled, and the rest is unlabeled. These algorithms leverage the labeled data to guide the learning process and make predictions on the unlabeled data. They are particularly useful when labeling large amounts of data is expensive or time-consuming.

4. Reinforcement Learning Algorithms: Reinforcement learning algorithms learn through trial and error by interacting with an environment. They receive feedback in the form of rewards or penalties based on their actions, allowing them to learn optimal strategies to maximize rewards over time. These algorithms are commonly used in applications such as robotics, gaming, and autonomous systems.

5. Deep Learning Algorithms: Deep learning algorithms are a subset of machine learning algorithms that utilize artificial neural networks with multiple hidden layers. These algorithms are designed to mimic the human brain's structure and function, enabling them to learn complex patterns and representations from large amounts of data. Deep learning algorithms have achieved remarkable success in various fields, including computer vision, natural language processing, and speech recognition.

Understanding the different types of machine learning algorithms is crucial for anyone interested in statistical modeling. Each algorithm has its own strengths and weaknesses, making it suitable for specific tasks and datasets. By familiarizing ourselves with these algorithms, we can leverage their capabilities to solve real-world problems and make data-driven decisions.

Importance of Statistical Modeling in Machine Learning

In today's digital age, machine learning has become an essential tool for businesses, researchers, and individuals alike. It has the power to analyze vast amounts of data, uncover patterns, make predictions, and automate decision-making processes. However, behind the scenes of machine learning lies the crucial aspect of statistical modeling, which plays a fundamental role in the accuracy, reliability, and interpretability of these models.

Statistical modeling is the backbone of machine learning, providing a framework for understanding and analyzing complex data sets. It encompasses a range of techniques that enable us to extract meaningful information from data, make informed predictions, and draw robust conclusions. By integrating statistical modeling into machine learning algorithms, we can enhance the performance and effectiveness of these models across various domains and applications.

One of the key reasons for the importance of statistical modeling in machine learning is its ability to handle uncertainty. Real-world data is often noisy, incomplete, and subject to various sources of error. Statistical modeling equips us with methods to quantify and manage these uncertainties, allowing us to make more reliable predictions and decisions. By understanding the underlying statistical properties of our data, we can assess the confidence in our model's predictions and make informed judgments about its reliability.

Furthermore, statistical modeling facilitates the interpretation and understanding of machine learning models. While complex algorithms such as deep learning can provide remarkable predictive accuracy, they often lack interpretability. Statistical modeling, on the other hand, allows us to characterize the relationships between variables, identify significant factors, and extract meaningful insights from the data. This interpretability is crucial, especially in applications where explanations and justifications are required, such as healthcare, finance, and legal domains.

Additionally, statistical modeling provides a systematic approach to model building and evaluation. It enables us to select appropriate variables, identify potential biases, test hypotheses, and assess model performance. By incorporating statistical principles into the machine learning workflow, we can ensure that our models are robust, unbiased, and accurately reflect the underlying data generating process.

In conclusion, statistical modeling is of utmost importance in machine learning as it enhances the accuracy, reliability, interpretability, and overall performance of these models. By embracing statistical techniques, we can effectively tackle uncertainty, interpret complex relationships, and build trustworthy models that can be applied across diverse domains. Whether you are a data scientist, a business professional, or simply someone interested in machine learning, understanding statistical modeling is essential for harnessing the full potential of this rapidly evolving field.

Chapter 2: Fundamentals of Statistical Modeling

Basics of Statistics

Statistics is a fundamental aspect of statistical modeling and plays a crucial role in various fields, including machine learning. It provides the tools and techniques necessary to analyze and interpret data, enabling us to make informed decisions and predictions. This subchapter aims to demystify the basics of statistics, making it accessible to everyone, regardless of their background in statistical modeling.

To begin with, statistics involves the collection, organization, analysis, interpretation, and presentation of data. It helps us understand the patterns, trends, and relationships within a dataset, allowing us to draw meaningful insights. Statistical modeling, on the other hand, is the process of creating mathematical models to represent and analyze real-world phenomena. It involves selecting an appropriate statistical technique based on the data and research question at hand.

In this subchapter, we will cover some fundamental concepts in statistics, starting with descriptive statistics. Descriptive statistics involves summarizing and describing the main features of a dataset. Measures such as mean, median, mode, variance, and standard deviation will be explained in simple terms, along with graphical representations like histograms and box plots.

Next, we will delve into inferential statistics, which allows us to draw conclusions or make predictions about a population based on a sample. Topics such as hypothesis testing, confidence intervals, and p-values will be explored, providing a solid foundation for understanding statistical significance and the reliability of our findings.

Furthermore, this subchapter will introduce probability theory, an essential component of statistics. Probability theory enables us to quantify uncertainty and make predictions based on the likelihood of different outcomes. Concepts like random variables, probability distributions, and the central limit theorem will be explained, emphasizing their relevance in statistical modeling.

Lastly, we will touch upon the importance of data visualization in statistics. Visual representations of data help us understand complex patterns more effectively and communicate our findings to others. Techniques such as scatter plots, bar charts, and heatmaps will be discussed, along with best practices for creating clear and informative visualizations.

By grasping the basics of statistics, readers will gain a solid understanding of statistical modeling concepts, empowering them to apply these techniques in various domains. Whether you are a data scientist, a business analyst, or simply someone interested in statistics, this subchapter will provide you with the necessary knowledge to navigate the world of statistical modeling.

Probability and Distributions

Probability and distributions form the foundation of statistical modeling and are essential concepts to understand in the field of machine learning. In this subchapter, we will demystify these concepts and explain their significance in statistical modeling, catering to an audience of EVERY ONE interested in the niche of Statistical Modeling.

Probability is the measure of the likelihood that an event will occur. It allows us to quantify uncertainty and make informed decisions based on data. Understanding probability is crucial for statistical modeling as it enables us to estimate the likelihood of different outcomes and make predictions. We will explore the basic principles of probability, including the laws of probability, conditional probability, and Bayes' theorem. By grasping these concepts, you will gain a solid understanding of probability and its role in statistical modeling.

Distributions, on the other hand, are mathematical functions that describe the likelihood of different outcomes in a dataset. They help us understand the patterns and characteristics of data, enabling us to make inferences and draw conclusions. We will delve into different types of distributions commonly used in statistical modeling, such as the normal distribution, binomial distribution, and Poisson distribution. By understanding these distributions, you will be equipped with the necessary tools to analyze and interpret data effectively.

Furthermore, we will explore how probability and distributions intertwine in statistical modeling. We will discuss how to use probability distributions to model real-world phenomena and make predictions. We will also introduce concepts like random variables, expected values, and variance, which are essential for understanding the behavior of data and creating accurate statistical models.

Throughout this subchapter, we will provide practical examples and intuitive explanations to make these complex concepts accessible to EVERY ONE interested in Statistical Modeling. We will also highlight the relevance of probability and distributions in different domains, such as finance, healthcare, and marketing. By the end of this subchapter, you will have a solid understanding of probability and distributions, empowering you to apply statistical modeling techniques in various real-world scenarios.

Demystifying Machine Learning: A Statistical Modeling Guide for Everyone aims to break down complex statistical concepts and make them accessible to EVERY ONE interested in the niche of Statistical Modeling. By providing clear explanations, practical examples, and real-world applications, this book equips readers with the necessary knowledge to effectively utilize statistical modeling techniques and contribute to the advancement of various industries. Whether you are a beginner or an experienced professional, this book will serve as a valuable resource in your journey towards mastering statistical modeling.

Hypothesis Testing and Confidence Intervals

In the world of statistical modeling, hypothesis testing and confidence intervals play a vital role in making informed decisions and drawing meaningful conclusions. These powerful tools allow us to assess the reliability of our findings and determine the significance of our results. In this subchapter, we will demystify the concepts of hypothesis testing and confidence intervals, empowering everyone, regardless of their background, to understand and utilize these techniques in their statistical modeling endeavors.

Hypothesis testing is a statistical method used to determine whether a certain claim or hypothesis about a population is likely to be true or not. It involves formulating a null hypothesis, which represents the claim being tested, and an alternative hypothesis, which contradicts the null hypothesis. By collecting and analyzing a sample from the population, we can assess the evidence against the null hypothesis and make an inference about the entire population.

Confidence intervals, on the other hand, provide a range of plausible values for an unknown population parameter. They are constructed using sample data and provide an estimate of the population parameter along with a measure of uncertainty. Confidence intervals help us understand the precision of our estimates and evaluate the potential range of values within which the parameter is likely to exist.

Understanding hypothesis testing and confidence intervals is crucial for everyone involved in statistical modeling. Whether you are a data scientist, a business analyst, or simply someone interested in understanding the world through data, these concepts allow you to make evidence-based decisions and draw meaningful conclusions. By grasping the fundamentals of hypothesis testing and confidence intervals, you can become more confident in your statistical analyses and communicate your findings effectively.

In this subchapter, we will explore the step-by-step process of hypothesis testing, including defining the null and alternative hypotheses, selecting an appropriate significance level, calculating test statistics, and interpreting the results. We will also delve into confidence intervals, discussing their construction, interpretation, and the factors that affect their width.

By the end of this subchapter, you will have a solid foundation in hypothesis testing and confidence intervals, enabling you to confidently apply these techniques in your statistical modeling endeavors. Whether you are studying the effects of a new drug, analyzing customer behavior, or exploring the impact of marketing campaigns, hypothesis testing and confidence intervals will be your guiding light in making data-driven decisions. So, let's demystify these concepts and unlock the power of statistical modeling for everyone.

Chapter 3: Supervised Learning Techniques

Linear Regression

Linear regression is a fundamental statistical modeling technique that plays a vital role in the field of machine learning. It forms the basis for understanding relationships between variables and making predictions based on these relationships. In this subchapter, we will demystify linear regression and explain its practical applications in statistical modeling.

At its core, linear regression is a statistical approach for modeling the relationship between a dependent variable and one or more independent variables. The technique assumes a linear relationship between the variables, where a change in one variable corresponds to a proportional change in the other. By fitting a line to the data points, linear regression enables us to estimate the value of the dependent variable based on the independent variables.

Linear regression has a wide range of applications across various domains, making it an essential tool in statistical modeling. For example, in finance, linear regression can be used to predict stock prices based on historical data. In marketing, it can help estimate the impact of advertising on sales. In healthcare, it can assist in predicting patient outcomes based on various medical factors. These applications highlight the versatility and significance of linear regression in real-world scenarios.

To perform linear regression, we employ various statistical techniques, such as least squares estimation, to find the best-fitting line that minimizes the sum of the squared differences between the predicted and actual values. The resulting line represents the regression equation, which can be used to make predictions and draw insights from the data. Additionally, the statistical significance of the regression coefficients can be determined to understand the strength and direction of the relationships between the variables.

Understanding the assumptions of linear regression is crucial to ensure accurate modeling. These assumptions include linearity, independence of errors, homoscedasticity, and normality of residuals. Violating these assumptions may lead to biased or unreliable results. Therefore, it is essential to assess and validate these assumptions before drawing conclusions from the regression analysis.

In this subchapter, we will delve deeper into the concepts of linear regression, exploring topics such as simple linear regression, multiple linear regression, and interpreting regression coefficients. We will also discuss techniques for model evaluation and diagnostics, such as residual analysis and goodness of fit measures.

By the end of this subchapter, you will have a solid understanding of linear regression and its practical applications in statistical modeling. Whether you are a data scientist, researcher, or someone interested in the field of machine learning, this knowledge will empower you to leverage linear regression for insightful analysis and informed decision-making. So let's embark on this journey of demystifying linear regression and unlock its potential in the world of statistical modeling.

Logistic Regression

Logistic regression is a fundamental statistical modeling technique that plays a crucial role in the field of machine learning. It is a powerful tool used to predict the probability of an event occurring based on various input variables. In this subchapter, we will demystify the concept of logistic regression and explore its applications in statistical modeling.

At its core, logistic regression is a binary classification algorithm that is widely used in diverse domains such as healthcare, finance, marketing, and social sciences. The goal of logistic regression is to estimate the probability of an event happening by fitting a logistic function to a set of input variables. Unlike linear regression, which predicts continuous values, logistic regression predicts the probability of an event falling into one of two categories (e.g., yes or no, true or false). It is particularly useful when dealing with categorical or binary outcomes.

In this subchapter, we will delve into the mathematical foundations of logistic regression, explaining how it transforms a linear model into a sigmoidal function that maps the input variables to the probability of the event occurring. We will discuss the concept of odds ratios and how they relate to the coefficients of the logistic regression model. We will also explore the importance of interpreting these coefficients in terms of their impact on the probability of the event.

Moreover, we will cover various techniques for model evaluation and selection, including assessing the goodness-of-fit, understanding the significance of predictors, and dealing with issues such as multicollinearity. We will discuss the use of regularization techniques like L1 and L2 regularization to prevent overfitting and improve the generalizability of the logistic regression model.

Throughout this subchapter, we will provide practical examples and real-world case studies to illustrate the application of logistic regression in statistical modeling. We will demonstrate how logistic regression can be used to solve problems such as predicting customer churn, identifying the likelihood of diseases, or classifying sentiment in text data.

By the end of this subchapter, readers will have a comprehensive understanding of logistic regression, its mathematical underpinnings, and its utility in statistical modeling. Whether you are a beginner in the field of machine learning or an experienced data scientist, this subchapter will equip you with the necessary knowledge to apply logistic regression effectively in your own projects.

Decision Trees

In the realm of statistical modeling, decision trees are powerful and versatile tools that have gained significant popularity in recent years. This subchapter aims to demystify decision trees and provide a comprehensive understanding of their applications and benefits for everyone interested in statistical modeling.

Decision trees are a fundamental part of machine learning and are widely used for both classification and regression tasks. They are graphical models that represent a series of decisions or rules that lead to a predicted outcome or target variable. This graphical representation resembles a tree, where each internal node represents a feature or attribute, each branch represents a decision, and each leaf node represents the outcome or prediction.

One of the key advantages of decision trees is their interpretability. Unlike other complex models, decision trees offer a transparent and intuitive representation of the decision-making process. This makes them particularly useful for understanding and explaining the underlying patterns and relationships within the data. Decision trees can be easily visualized, allowing users to grasp the decision paths and the importance of each feature in the prediction.

Furthermore, decision trees are non-parametric models, meaning they make no assumptions about the distribution of the data. This flexibility enables decision trees to handle a variety of data types, including categorical, numerical, and mixed variables. Decision trees are also robust to outliers and missing data, which makes them versatile in real-world scenarios where data quality may vary.

Another significant advantage of decision trees is their ability to handle interactions between variables. By splitting the data based on the values of different features at each internal node, decision trees can capture complex interactions and nonlinear relationships that exist within the data. This makes decision trees particularly useful when dealing with high-dimensional datasets or when interactions between features are suspected to be influential.

In conclusion, decision trees are a valuable addition to the toolkit of statistical modeling. Their interpretability, flexibility, and capability to capture complex interactions make them suitable for a wide range of applications. Whether you are a beginner or an experienced practitioner in the field of statistical modeling, understanding decision trees and their applications is essential for harnessing the power of machine learning in your data analysis endeavors.

Random Forests

Random Forests is a popular and powerful machine learning algorithm that falls under the umbrella of statistical modeling. It is widely used for solving a variety of problems across different fields, making it an essential tool for anyone interested in statistical modeling.

At its core, Random Forests is an ensemble learning method that combines multiple decision trees to make predictions. It is called "random" because each decision tree is trained on a random subset of the data and features, introducing randomness into the model. This randomness helps to reduce overfitting and improve the model's generalization ability.

The strength of Random Forests lies in its ability to handle both classification and regression tasks with high accuracy. By aggregating the predictions of individual decision trees, the algorithm can provide robust and reliable results. Moreover, it can handle large datasets with numerous features without requiring extensive pre-processing or feature engineering.

One of the key advantages of Random Forests is its interpretability. Unlike black-box models like neural networks, Random Forests allow us to understand the importance of each feature in the prediction process. By examining the feature importances, we can gain valuable insights into the underlying relationships and patterns within the data.

Further, Random Forests can handle missing values and outliers effectively, making it a valuable tool for real-world datasets that often contain imperfections. The algorithm's ability to handle missing values reduces the need for data imputation techniques, simplifying the modeling process.

In addition to its predictive power, Random Forests can also provide valuable insights into the relationships between variables. By analyzing the decision trees within the ensemble, we can identify interactions and dependencies among the features, aiding in feature selection and engineering.

Overall, Random Forests offer a versatile and accessible approach to statistical modeling for everyone interested in machine learning. Its combination of accuracy, interpretability, and robustness make it a go-to algorithm for a wide range of applications. Whether you are a beginner or an experienced practitioner in statistical modeling, understanding and utilizing Random Forests can undoubtedly enhance your modeling capabilities and provide valuable insights from your data.

Support Vector Machines

Support Vector Machines (SVM) are a powerful and widely used algorithm in the field of statistical modeling. They are particularly useful when dealing with complex and high-dimensional data. In this subchapter, we will demystify Support Vector Machines and explain how they work in a simple and accessible manner.

Support Vector Machines are a type of supervised learning algorithm that can be used for classification and regression tasks. The main idea behind SVM is to find the optimal hyperplane that separates the data points into different classes, maximizing the margin between the classes. The hyperplane is defined as the line or surface that best separates the data points in a higher-dimensional space.

One of the key advantages of Support Vector Machines is their ability to handle nonlinear relationships by using a technique called kernel trick. The kernel trick allows SVM to transform the data into a higher-dimensional space where a linear separation is possible. This enables SVM to capture complex patterns and make accurate predictions.

To find the optimal hyperplane, Support Vector Machines use a mathematical optimization algorithm called Quadratic Programming. This algorithm aims to minimize the error rate while maximizing the margin between the classes. The data points that lie on the margin or are misclassified are called support vectors, hence the name Support Vector Machines.

Support Vector Machines have several advantages over other classification algorithms. They are robust against overfitting and can handle large datasets efficiently. Additionally, SVM can handle both numerical and categorical data, making them versatile for various types of problems.

In practical applications, Support Vector Machines have been successfully used in a wide range of fields, including image recognition, text classification, and bioinformatics. They have also been applied to financial modeling, fraud detection, and customer segmentation.

Although Support Vector Machines can be complex to understand at first, with this subchapter, we aim to demystify the underlying concepts and provide a clear understanding of how SVM works. By demystifying Support Vector Machines, we hope to make statistical modeling accessible to everyone, regardless of their background or expertise.

In conclusion, Support Vector Machines are a powerful algorithm in statistical modeling that can handle complex and high-dimensional data. With their ability to find optimal hyperplanes and handle nonlinear relationships, SVM has become an essential tool in various fields. By understanding the underlying principles of Support Vector Machines, you can unlock their potential and apply them to a wide range of problems in statistical modeling.

Chapter 4: Unsupervised Learning Techniques

Clustering Algorithms

In the world of statistical modeling, clustering algorithms play a crucial role in uncovering patterns and relationships within data. Clustering refers to the process of grouping similar data points together based on their inherent characteristics. This subchapter will demystify clustering algorithms, shedding light on their significance and how they are applied in various domains.

Clustering algorithms are widely used in fields such as marketing, biology, finance, and social sciences, among others. Their primary goal is to identify groups or clusters of data points that share similar attributes or behaviors. This allows researchers and analysts to gain insights into the underlying structure of the data and make informed decisions.

One popular clustering algorithm is k-means clustering, which partitions the data into k distinct clusters based on their proximity to centroids. It is an iterative algorithm that assigns data points to clusters based on their distance from the centroids, recalculating the centroids after each iteration. K-means clustering is efficient and works well on large datasets, making it a valuable tool for various applications.

Another commonly used clustering algorithm is hierarchical clustering. This algorithm builds a hierarchy of clusters by merging or splitting them based on their similarity. It starts with individual data points and gradually creates clusters, forming a tree-like structure called a dendrogram. Hierarchical clustering provides a visual representation of the clustering process and helps identify the optimal number of clusters.

Density-based clustering algorithms, such as DBSCAN (Density-Based Spatial Clustering of Applications with Noise), are useful for identifying clusters of arbitrary shapes. Unlike k-means or hierarchical clustering, density-based algorithms do not require specifying the number of clusters in advance. Instead, they identify regions of high density as clusters and separate noise points from the clusters.

Clustering algorithms have numerous applications. In marketing, they can be used to segment customers based on their preferences and behaviors, allowing businesses to tailor their marketing strategies accordingly. In biology, clustering can help identify genes that exhibit similar expression patterns, leading to a better understanding of biological processes. In finance, clustering algorithms can assist in portfolio management and risk assessment by grouping similar stocks or assets.

In conclusion, clustering algorithms are powerful tools in statistical modeling that enable researchers and analysts to discover patterns and relationships within data. With their ability to group similar data points together, clustering algorithms find applications in various domains such as marketing, biology, finance, and social sciences. By demystifying clustering algorithms, this subchapter aims to equip everyone with a fundamental understanding of their significance and potential applications in statistical modeling.

Dimensionality Reduction Techniques

Dimensionality reduction is a crucial concept in the field of statistical modeling and machine learning. As datasets continue to grow in size and complexity, it becomes increasingly important to find ways to simplify and represent the data in a more manageable form. This is where dimensionality reduction techniques come into play.

Dimensionality reduction refers to the process of reducing the number of variables or features in a dataset while still retaining the most important and relevant information. By doing so, we can reduce the computational requirements, improve model performance, and gain a better understanding of the underlying patterns and relationships within the data.

There are several popular dimensionality reduction techniques that are widely used in statistical modeling. One such technique is Principal Component Analysis (PCA). PCA is a linear transformation method that identifies the directions (principal components) along which the data varies the most. It then projects the data onto these components, effectively reducing the dimensionality while preserving the maximum amount of variation.

Another commonly used technique is t-distributed Stochastic Neighbor Embedding (t-SNE). Unlike PCA, t-SNE is a non-linear technique that aims to preserve the local structure of the data. It is particularly useful for visualizing high-dimensional data in lower-dimensional spaces, making it a valuable tool for exploratory data analysis.

Other dimensionality reduction techniques include Linear Discriminant Analysis (LDA), which is often used in classification problems to find the best discriminative features, and Autoencoders, which are neural networks designed to learn efficient data representations by encoding and decoding the data.

It is important to note that dimensionality reduction is not a one-size-fits-all solution. The choice of technique depends on the specific problem at hand and the nature of the data. It is crucial to assess the trade-offs between dimensionality reduction and potential loss of information, as well as the impact on downstream modeling tasks.

In conclusion, dimensionality reduction techniques are valuable tools in the field of statistical modeling. They allow us to simplify complex datasets, improve computational efficiency, and gain insights into the underlying structure of the data. Whether you are a beginner or an experienced practitioner in statistical modeling, understanding and applying dimensionality reduction techniques will undoubtedly enhance your ability to effectively analyze and model large and high-dimensional datasets.

Principal Component Analysis

Principal Component Analysis (PCA) is a powerful technique in statistical modeling that is widely used in various fields, ranging from finance and marketing to biology and computer science. In this subchapter, we will demystify the concept of PCA and explore its applications, making it accessible to everyone interested in statistical modeling.

PCA is a dimensionality reduction technique that allows us to transform a large set of variables into a smaller set of uncorrelated variables, known as principal components. These principal components capture the maximum amount of variation in the original data, making them ideal for data exploration and visualization. By reducing the dimensionality of the data, PCA helps in simplifying complex data sets and extracting meaningful information.

One of the key benefits of PCA is its ability to identify the most important features or variables in a dataset. It achieves this by ranking the principal components based on the amount of variation they explain. By considering only the top-ranked components, we can effectively reduce the dimensionality of the data without losing much information. This is particularly useful when dealing with high-dimensional data, where traditional statistical techniques may struggle to provide meaningful insights.

PCA can also be used for data preprocessing and denoising. By removing the least significant principal components, which are associated with noise or irrelevant features, we can enhance the signal-to-noise ratio and improve the performance of subsequent modeling algorithms. This is especially valuable in applications such as image and signal processing.

Furthermore, PCA enables us to visualize high-dimensional data in a lower-dimensional space. By plotting the data points using the first two or three principal components, we can gain insights into the structure and patterns present in the data. This visualization technique is particularly helpful when dealing with large datasets, as it allows us to explore and interpret the data more easily.

In summary, Principal Component Analysis is a fundamental tool in statistical modeling that helps in dimensionality reduction, feature selection, data preprocessing, denoising, and data visualization. Its versatility and widespread applications make it an essential technique for anyone interested in exploring and understanding complex data sets. Whether you are a student, researcher, or practitioner in the field of statistical modeling, PCA is a valuable addition to your analytical toolkit.

K-means Clustering

In the world of statistical modeling, one of the most commonly used techniques is known as K-means clustering. This powerful tool allows us to group similar data points together, enabling us to draw meaningful insights from complex datasets. Whether you are a seasoned data scientist or a curious individual interested in statistical modeling, understanding the concept of K-means clustering is essential.

K-means clustering is an unsupervised learning algorithm that aims to partition a given dataset into K distinct clusters, where K represents the number of clusters specified by the user. The algorithm achieves this by iteratively assigning each data point to the nearest centroid and then recalculating the centroid based on the newly formed clusters. This process continues until the algorithm converges and the centroids stabilize.

The beauty of K-means clustering lies in its simplicity and efficiency. It can be applied to a wide range of applications, including customer segmentation, image compression, anomaly detection, and more. By grouping similar data points together, K-means clustering helps us uncover patterns and relationships that may not be immediately apparent.

To illustrate the power of K-means clustering, let's consider a hypothetical scenario. Imagine we have a dataset containing information about customers' purchasing behavior. By applying K-means clustering, we can divide our customers into distinct segments based on their buying patterns. This segmentation allows us to tailor marketing strategies to each group specifically, increasing customer satisfaction and driving sales.

However, it's important to note that while K-means clustering is a valuable technique, it also has limitations. It assumes that clusters are spherical and equally sized, which may not always be the case in real-world scenarios. Additionally, determining the optimal number of clusters (K value) can be challenging and requires careful consideration.

In conclusion, K-means clustering is a fundamental tool in statistical modeling that allows us to uncover hidden patterns and relationships within complex datasets. Its simplicity and efficiency make it accessible to individuals interested in statistical modeling, regardless of their background. By leveraging the power of K-means clustering, we can gain valuable insights and make informed decisions that drive success in various domains, from business to healthcare and beyond.

Hierarchical Clustering

Hierarchical clustering is a powerful technique used in statistical modeling to uncover patterns and relationships within data. It is a popular method for grouping similar objects or observations together based on their similarities or dissimilarities. In this subchapter, we will explore the concept of hierarchical clustering and its applications in statistical modeling.

Hierarchical clustering works on the principle of building a hierarchy of clusters. It starts by considering each data point as a separate cluster and then iteratively merges the clusters based on their similarity. The clustering process continues until all the data points are merged into a single cluster or until a stopping criterion is met.

One of the key advantages of hierarchical clustering is that it provides a visual representation of the clustering results through dendrograms. A dendrogram is a tree-like structure that shows the hierarchical relationships among the clusters. It allows us to interpret the clustering results and understand the similarities and dissimilarities between different clusters.

Hierarchical clustering can be applied in various domains of statistical modeling. For example, in market segmentation, it can be used to identify distinct customer segments based on their purchasing behaviors or demographic characteristics. In genetics, it can be used to cluster genes based on their expression levels, helping researchers understand the underlying biological processes.

Another application of hierarchical clustering is in image analysis. It can be used to group similar images together, enabling tasks such as image classification or object recognition. By identifying clusters of similar images, we can build more accurate models and improve the performance of machine learning algorithms.

In addition to its applications, hierarchical clustering also offers flexibility in choosing the similarity measure and linkage criteria. The similarity measure defines how the similarity or dissimilarity between two clusters is calculated, while the linkage criteria determine how the clusters are merged. The choice of these parameters depends on the specific problem and the nature of the data.

In conclusion, hierarchical clustering is a valuable tool in statistical modeling that allows us to uncover patterns and relationships within data. Its ability to provide a visual representation of the clustering results and its diverse applications make it an essential technique for data analysis. By understanding the concept and applications of hierarchical clustering, we can gain valuable insights and improve decision-making in various domains of statistical modeling.

Chapter 5: Evaluation and Validation of Models

Splitting Data into Training and Testing Sets

In the realm of statistical modeling, one of the fundamental steps in building a robust machine learning model is to split the available data into training and testing sets. This process allows us to evaluate the performance and generalization capabilities of our models. In this subchapter, we will delve into the importance of splitting data and provide practical guidelines for doing so effectively.

Why is splitting data into training and testing sets crucial? Well, when we develop a machine learning model, we want it to be able to accurately predict outcomes for unseen data, not just the data it was trained on. By splitting the data, we can simulate this scenario by training the model on a subset of the available data and then testing it on a separate, unseen subset.

The question arises: how should we split our data? There is no one-size-fits-all answer, as it depends on various factors such as the dataset size, the complexity of the problem, and the available computational resources. However, a common approach is to allocate around 70-80% of the data for training and the remaining 20-30% for testing.

It is crucial to ensure that the splitting process is random and representative of the overall dataset. Randomness helps to avoid bias and ensures that the training and testing sets have similar statistical properties. For instance, if we are working with a dataset that has class imbalance (i.e., one class is significantly more prevalent than others), we should strive to maintain the same class distribution in both sets.

To facilitate the splitting process, various libraries and tools provide built-in functions. For example, in Python, scikit-learn's `train_test_split` function can be used to randomly split the data into training and testing sets with just a few lines of code. This makes the process more accessible to everyone, even those without an extensive background in programming.

By splitting the data into training and testing sets, we can evaluate the model's performance on unseen data, which is a critical step in statistical modeling. It allows us to assess the model's ability to generalize and identify potential issues such as overfitting or underfitting. Furthermore, it enables us to fine-tune the model parameters and evaluate different algorithms or approaches.

In conclusion, splitting data into training and testing sets is an essential aspect of statistical modeling. It provides a way to evaluate the performance and generalization capabilities of machine learning models. By following the guidelines outlined in this subchapter, you can ensure that your model is trained and evaluated on representative and unbiased data, leading to more accurate and reliable results.

Cross-Validation Techniques

In the world of statistical modeling, cross-validation techniques play a crucial role in evaluating and fine-tuning machine learning models. These techniques help us understand the performance, generalizability, and robustness of our models. Whether you are a beginner or an expert in statistical modeling, understanding cross-validation is essential for building accurate and reliable models.

Cross-validation is a statistical method used to estimate how well a model will perform on unseen data. It involves partitioning the available data into multiple subsets, training the model on one subset, and evaluating its performance on the remaining subset. This process is repeated multiple times, with different subsets serving as the training and evaluation data, providing a more comprehensive assessment of the model's performance.

One of the most widely used cross-validation techniques is k-fold cross-validation. In this technique, the data is divided into k equally sized subsets or folds. The model is trained on k-1 folds and evaluated on the remaining fold. This process is repeated k times, with each fold serving as the evaluation set once. The final performance metric is the average of the evaluation results from all k iterations. K-fold cross-validation helps in obtaining a more stable and reliable estimate of the model's performance, as it uses the entire dataset for training and evaluation.

Another cross-validation technique is stratified cross-validation, which ensures that the class distribution in the training and evaluation sets remains consistent. This is particularly useful when dealing with imbalanced datasets where the number of instances belonging to different classes differs significantly. By maintaining the same class distribution in each fold, stratified cross-validation provides a more representative evaluation of the model's performance.

Leave-one-out cross-validation (LOOCV) is another technique commonly used when dealing with small datasets. In LOOCV, each data point is treated as a separate fold, with the model trained on all but one data point and evaluated on the left-out point. This technique provides a more precise evaluation but can be computationally expensive for large datasets.

Cross-validation techniques are invaluable tools for assessing the quality of machine learning models and selecting the best ones for deployment. By using these techniques, we can ensure that our models are robust, generalizable, and perform well on unseen data. Whether you are a beginner or an expert in statistical modeling, understanding and utilizing cross-validation techniques will significantly enhance your model building process.

Model Evaluation Metrics

In the realm of statistical modeling, the evaluation of machine learning models is a critical step in determining their effectiveness and reliability. Model evaluation metrics provide a systematic way to assess the performance of these models and make informed decisions based on their outcomes. This subchapter aims to demystify the various evaluation metrics commonly used in statistical modeling, catering to a diverse audience interested in understanding the intricacies of machine learning.

Evaluation metrics serve as a yardstick to measure the accuracy, precision, recall, and overall performance of machine learning models. They help answer crucial questions such as: How well does the model predict outcomes? Does it suffer from overfitting or underfitting? Are there any biases or errors in the predictions? By comprehending these metrics, individuals can make informed judgments about the effectiveness of machine learning models and identify areas for improvement.

The subchapter begins by introducing the fundamental evaluation metrics, such as accuracy, precision, and recall. These metrics provide a holistic view of model performance by quantifying the correct predictions, false positives, and false negatives made by the model. We delve into the intricacies of these metrics, discussing their strengths, weaknesses, and suitable use cases.

Moving forward, the subchapter explores advanced evaluation metrics, including the F1 score, area under the receiver operating characteristic curve (AUC-ROC), and mean squared error (MSE).

These metrics provide a more nuanced understanding of model performance by considering factors such as class imbalance, prediction probabilities, and regression analysis. We explain how these metrics can be used to evaluate different types of machine learning models, from classification to regression.

To further enhance the comprehension of model evaluation, the subchapter also discusses the concept of model validation and cross-validation techniques. These techniques help estimate the true performance of a model on unseen data, providing a more reliable assessment of its generalizability and robustness.

By the end of this subchapter, readers will have gained a comprehensive understanding of model evaluation metrics and their significance in statistical modeling. Armed with this knowledge, they will be equipped to evaluate and compare machine learning models effectively, regardless of their background or expertise. Whether you are a data scientist, a business professional, or simply curious about the world of statistical modeling, this subchapter will empower you to make informed decisions and harness the power of machine learning for various applications.

Chapter 6: Feature Engineering and Selection

Importance of Feature Engineering

In the realm of statistical modeling and machine learning, feature engineering plays a pivotal role in transforming raw data into meaningful representations that can be effectively utilized by algorithms. This subchapter aims to demystify the concept of feature engineering and highlight its significance in building accurate and robust models.

Feature engineering refers to the process of selecting, creating, and transforming variables or features from the available data to improve the performance of machine learning algorithms. The quality and relevance of the features directly impact the model's ability to generalize well, make accurate predictions, and uncover important patterns and relationships within the data.

Effective feature engineering involves a deep understanding of the problem domain, the data at hand, and the algorithms being employed. It requires domain knowledge and creativity to identify the most informative variables and construct new features that capture the underlying patterns and relationships in the data.

One of the primary reasons why feature engineering is crucial is that raw data often contains noise, irrelevant variables, or missing values. By carefully selecting and transforming variables, feature engineering helps in reducing noise, removing redundant or irrelevant information, and filling in missing values. This, in turn, enhances the performance of models by reducing overfitting and improving generalization to unseen data.

Furthermore, feature engineering allows us to extract more meaningful information from the data, making it easier for machine learning algorithms to identify complex patterns and relationships. By creating new features based on domain knowledge or statistical techniques, we can provide the model with more discriminative information, enabling it to make better predictions.

Feature engineering also enables us to handle different types of data, such as categorical, numerical, or textual. It involves techniques like one-hot encoding, binning, scaling, and text preprocessing, which convert raw data into a format that is compatible with the algorithms being used. This ensures that the models can effectively utilize the information contained in the data, regardless of its type or format.

In summary, feature engineering is a critical step in the statistical modeling process, as it helps in transforming raw data into meaningful representations that enhance the performance and accuracy of machine learning algorithms. By carefully selecting, creating, and transforming features, we can reduce noise, handle missing values, extract more informative aspects of the data, and make it easier for models to uncover hidden patterns and relationships. In essence, feature engineering is the art of molding data to optimize the learning process and empower statistical models to make accurate predictions and valuable insights for everyone.

Feature Extraction Techniques

Feature extraction is a fundamental step in statistical modeling and machine learning. It involves transforming raw data into a set of meaningful features that can be used to train models and make predictions. In this subchapter, we will explore various feature extraction techniques that are widely used in the field.

One of the most common feature extraction techniques is principal component analysis (PCA). PCA is a dimensionality reduction method that identifies the most important features in a dataset. By projecting the data onto a lower-dimensional space, PCA can capture the maximum amount of variance in the data. This technique is particularly useful when dealing with high-dimensional datasets, as it helps to eliminate noise and redundant information.

Another popular technique is feature scaling. Feature scaling involves transforming the numerical features in a dataset to a common scale. This is important because many machine learning algorithms are sensitive to the scale of the input features. Common scaling techniques include standardization, where the features are transformed to have zero mean and unit variance, and normalization, where the features are scaled to a specific range, such as [0, 1].

Feature extraction can also involve transforming categorical variables into numerical representations. One such technique is one-hot encoding, where each category is represented by a binary vector. This allows the categorical information to be incorporated into the modeling process. Another technique is target encoding, where each category is replaced with the mean or median of the target variable for that category. This can be particularly useful when dealing with high-cardinality categorical variables.

Furthermore, text data often requires specialized feature extraction techniques. One approach is to use bag-of-words, where each document is represented by a vector that counts the occurrence of each word. Another technique is term frequency-inverse document frequency (TF-IDF), which assigns weights to words based on their frequency in the document and their rarity across the entire corpus. These techniques enable the modeling of text data in a numerical format.

In conclusion, feature extraction techniques play a crucial role in statistical modeling and machine learning. They help to transform raw data into a format that can be effectively used by models. By understanding and applying these techniques, practitioners can improve the performance and interpretability of their models.

Feature Selection Methods

Feature selection is a critical step in statistical modeling, allowing us to identify the most relevant and informative variables for our analysis. In this subchapter, we will explore various methods of feature selection that can be applied in the context of machine learning.

One commonly used method is the filter approach, which assesses the relevance of features based on their individual characteristics. This approach relies on statistical measures, such as correlation coefficients or information gain, to determine the predictive power of each feature. By ranking the features according to these measures, we can select the top variables for our model.

Another popular approach is wrapper methods, which evaluate feature subsets by training and testing machine learning algorithms on different combinations of variables. This method considers the interaction between features and their impact on the model's performance. Although computationally intensive, wrapper methods often result in improved accuracy compared to filter methods.

Embedded methods are an alternative approach that combines feature selection with the model building process. These methods incorporate feature selection within the algorithm itself, optimizing the model's performance while simultaneously selecting the most relevant variables. Examples of embedded methods include LASSO (Least Absolute Shrinkage and Selection Operator) and ridge regression.

Additionally, there are dimensionality reduction techniques, such as Principal Component Analysis (PCA) and Singular Value Decomposition (SVD), which transform the original features into a lower-dimensional representation. These methods identify new variables, known as principal components, which capture the maximum amount of information from the original dataset. By selecting the principal components that explain the most variance, we can effectively reduce the dimensionality of the problem while retaining the most critical information.

It is important to note that the choice of feature selection method depends on the specific problem at hand and the characteristics of the dataset. While some methods are more suitable for high-dimensional data, others may be more effective for datasets with a smaller number of features. Experimentation and evaluation of different methods are crucial to determine the optimal approach for a given statistical modeling task.

In conclusion, feature selection methods play a vital role in statistical modeling by identifying the most relevant variables for analysis. Whether through filter, wrapper, embedded methods, or dimensionality reduction techniques, the goal is to improve model performance, reduce computational complexity, and enhance interpretability. By understanding and implementing these methods, we can effectively harness the power of machine learning and make informed decisions across various domains, from healthcare to finance, and beyond.

Handling Missing Data

In the world of statistical modeling, missing data is a common challenge that researchers and analysts face. Missing data refers to the absence of certain observations or values in a dataset, which can occur for various reasons such as non-response, data entry errors, or technical issues. Dealing with missing data is crucial to ensure accurate and reliable statistical modeling results.

This subchapter aims to demystify the complexities associated with missing data and provide practical strategies for handling this issue effectively. Whether you are a beginner or an experienced practitioner in statistical modeling, understanding how to handle missing data is essential for producing robust and meaningful results.

The subchapter begins by explaining the different types of missing data and their implications on statistical modeling. It discusses the distinction between missing completely at random (MCAR), missing at random (MAR), and missing not at random (MNAR) mechanisms, highlighting the importance of identifying the underlying missing data mechanism before choosing an appropriate analysis method.

Next, the subchapter delves into various techniques for handling missing data. It presents traditional approaches such as complete case analysis and pairwise deletion, along with their limitations and potential biases. It then introduces more advanced methods like multiple imputation, maximum likelihood estimation, and expectation-maximization algorithm, which offer more robust and accurate solutions to missing data problems.

Furthermore, the subchapter provides practical guidance on how to assess the extent and patterns of missing data in a dataset. It emphasizes the importance of conducting missing data analysis to gain insights into the missingness patterns and potential biases that may arise due to missing data.

To address the needs of a diverse audience, the subchapter also covers software tools and packages commonly used for handling missing data in statistical modeling. It provides step-by-step examples and code snippets using popular statistical software such as R and Python, enabling readers to implement the discussed techniques in their own projects.

By the end of this subchapter, readers will have a comprehensive understanding of the challenges posed by missing data in statistical modeling and will be equipped with a range of techniques to handle this issue effectively. Whether you are a researcher, analyst, or a curious individual, the knowledge gained from this subchapter will empower you to confidently handle missing data and produce reliable statistical modeling results.

Chapter 7: Model Interpretability and Explainability

Interpreting Linear Models

Linear models are one of the fundamental tools in statistical modeling, widely used across various fields to understand relationships between variables. In this subchapter, we will delve into the art of interpreting linear models and uncover the valuable insights they provide. Whether you are a seasoned statistician or just beginning your journey into statistical modeling, understanding how to interpret linear models is crucial for extracting meaningful information.

At its core, a linear model represents the relationship between a dependent variable and one or more independent variables using a straight line. This simple yet powerful model allows us to estimate the effect of each independent variable on the dependent variable. However, interpreting the coefficients of a linear model and understanding their significance can be a complex task.

One common interpretation of linear models is through the slope coefficient, which represents the change in the dependent variable for a unit change in the independent variable, holding all other variables constant. This interpretation provides insights into the direction and magnitude of the relationship. For example, if the slope coefficient of a variable is positive, it indicates that an increase in that variable leads to an increase in the dependent variable.

Another important aspect of interpreting linear models is assessing the statistical significance of the coefficients. Statistical significance helps determine if the relationship between the independent and dependent variables is real or simply due to chance. By examining the p-values associated with each coefficient, we can determine if the relationships observed in the data are statistically significant.

However, interpreting linear models goes beyond just coefficients and p-values. It involves understanding the context and limitations of the model, as well as assessing the goodness of fit. Goodness of fit measures, such as R-squared, provide a measure of how well the model fits the data. They give insights into the proportion of variance in the dependent variable that can be explained by the independent variables.

In this subchapter, we will explore various techniques and graphical tools that aid in interpreting linear models. We will discuss how to interpret interactions between variables, assess model assumptions, and handle outliers. Additionally, we will touch upon the importance of model validation and how to effectively communicate the results obtained from linear models.

By mastering the art of interpreting linear models, you will be equipped with the skills necessary to analyze relationships, make predictions, and draw meaningful conclusions from your data. Whether you are a researcher, data scientist, or simply someone interested in statistical modeling, this subchapter will guide you in demystifying the intricacies of linear models and enable you to harness their power in understanding real-world phenomena.

Explaining Black-Box Models

In the realm of statistical modeling, black-box models have gained significant popularity in recent years. These models, known for their complex and opaque nature, have become an integral part of machine learning algorithms. However, understanding how they work and interpreting their predictions can be quite challenging. In this subchapter, we aim to demystify black-box models and provide a comprehensive explanation for everyone interested in statistical modeling.

Black-box models are algorithms that make predictions based on intricate mathematical calculations, often utilizing neural networks or deep learning architectures. Unlike traditional models, such as linear regression or decision trees, black-box models do not offer explicit insights into the underlying relationships between input variables and predictions. Instead, they rely on a vast number of interconnected nodes, weights, and biases to process information and generate results.

For the average person, comprehending the inner workings of black-box models may seem overwhelming. However, it is essential to grasp certain concepts to understand their limitations and potential biases. One crucial aspect to consider is the training data used to develop these models. Black-box models learn patterns and relationships from massive datasets, and their predictions heavily rely on the information contained within the training data. If the training data is biased or incomplete, it can lead to biased predictions.

To address the interpretability issue, various techniques have been developed to shed light on black-box models. One popular approach is the use of feature importance or variable attribution methods. These methods quantify the impact of each input variable on the model's predictions, providing insights into which variables are most influential. Another technique is the creation of surrogate models, which are simpler and more interpretable models trained to mimic the behavior of the black-box model. Surrogate models can help in understanding the decision-making process of the black-box model.

Additionally, efforts are being made to develop advanced visualization tools that make black-box models more accessible to a wider audience. These tools aim to provide interactive visualizations, allowing users to explore and understand the model's behavior. Such tools can help individuals identify patterns, outliers, and potential biases within the model's predictions, contributing to better comprehension and trust.

In conclusion, black-box models pose unique challenges in statistical modeling due to their complexity and lack of interpretability. However, understanding the limitations and techniques to unravel their inner workings is crucial for users of statistical models. By shedding light on black-box models through feature importance methods, surrogate models, and visualization tools, we can bridge the gap between complexity and interpretability, making statistical modeling more accessible to a broader audience.

Model Explainability Techniques

In the world of statistical modeling, machine learning algorithms have become increasingly popular due to their ability to uncover patterns and make predictions from vast amounts of data. However, as these algorithms become more complex, understanding how they arrive at their decisions becomes challenging. This lack of transparency can lead to skepticism and mistrust, especially in critical domains such as healthcare, finance, and law.

To address this issue, researchers and practitioners have developed various model explainability techniques. These techniques aim to shed light on the inner workings of machine learning models, providing insights into how they make predictions and why they behave the way they do. By demystifying the black box nature of these models, explainability techniques allow stakeholders to gain trust in the decision-making process and ensure fairness, ethics, and accountability.

One popular explainability technique is feature importance analysis. This approach examines the contribution of each input feature to the model's output. By quantifying the impact of each feature, stakeholders can understand which factors the model considers most influential in making predictions. This information can help identify biases or potential issues with the data and provide insights for feature engineering or decision-making processes.

Another technique is partial dependence plots, which illustrate the relationship between a specific input feature and the predicted outcome while holding other features constant. These plots provide a clear visualization of how changing a feature's value impacts the model's prediction. By analyzing these plots, stakeholders can gain a deeper understanding of how the model reacts to different inputs and identify non-linear relationships that may not be apparent from traditional statistical analysis.

Additionally, model-agnostic techniques such as LIME (Local Interpretable Model-agnostic Explanations) and SHAP (SHapley Additive exPlanations) offer a general framework for explaining any machine learning model. LIME generates locally interpretable explanations by perturbing the input data and examining how the model's predictions change. SHAP, on the other hand, uses game theory concepts to assign importance values to each feature based on their contribution to the prediction. These techniques provide valuable insights into individual predictions and help build trust in the model's overall performance.

In conclusion, model explainability techniques play a vital role in the field of statistical modeling, allowing stakeholders to understand and trust machine learning models. From feature importance analysis to partial dependence plots and model-agnostic techniques like LIME and SHAP, these techniques provide insights into the decision-making process, uncover biases, and ensure fairness and accountability. By embracing model explainability, we can demystify machine learning and make it accessible to everyone, fostering a more transparent and trustworthy approach to statistical modeling.

Chapter 8: Model Optimization and Hyperparameter Tuning

Grid Search

One of the fundamental challenges in statistical modeling is finding the optimal set of parameters for a given model. This process, known as parameter tuning, is crucial for achieving the best possible performance and accuracy in machine learning tasks. Grid search is a widely used method for exploring different combinations of parameter values, helping to identify the optimal configuration for a model.

In grid search, we specify a grid of possible parameter values for each parameter of interest. The grid is defined by a set of discrete values or a range of values to be explored. The algorithm then systematically evaluates the model's performance for each combination of parameter values on the grid, selecting the configuration that yields the highest performance.

The main advantage of grid search is its simplicity and comprehensiveness. It exhaustively searches through all possible parameter combinations, ensuring that no potential configuration is overlooked. This approach is particularly useful when the relationship between the parameters and the model's performance is not well understood or when there are no intuitive starting points for tuning.

To illustrate the grid search process, let's consider an example. Suppose we have a classification problem and we are using a support vector machine (SVM) model. The key parameters we need to tune are the kernel type and the penalty parameter C. We define a grid of possible values for each parameter:

Kernel type: linear, polynomial, radial basis function (RBF)
C: 0.1, 1, 10

The grid search algorithm will evaluate the SVM model using each combination of the kernel type and C values. For example, it will fit the model with a linear kernel and C=0.1, then with a linear kernel and C=1, and so on. The evaluation can be based on a predetermined metric such as accuracy, precision, or recall.

Once all combinations have been evaluated, the grid search algorithm selects the configuration that yields the best performance metric. This configuration represents the optimal set of parameters for the model. By systematically exploring the parameter space, grid search helps us find the best combination for our specific modeling problem.

In conclusion, grid search is an essential technique in statistical modeling and machine learning. It enables us to systematically search through different combinations of parameter values, helping us find the optimal configuration for our models. By exhaustively exploring the parameter space, grid search ensures that we achieve the best possible performance, regardless of our level of understanding of the underlying relationships.

Randomized Search

In the world of statistical modeling and machine learning, finding the optimal set of hyperparameters for a model is often a challenging task. Hyperparameters are the configuration choices that are not learned by the model but need to be specified by the user. These choices greatly influence the model's performance and can have a significant impact on its accuracy and generalization capabilities.

One popular approach for tuning hyperparameters is grid search, where a predefined set of values is systematically explored. While grid search is a straightforward method, it can be computationally expensive and time-consuming, especially when dealing with a large number of hyperparameters and a wide range of possible values.

To overcome these limitations, an alternative method called randomized search has gained popularity among statisticians and machine learning practitioners. Randomized search follows a different philosophy, where hyperparameters are randomly sampled from a given distribution. This approach allows for a more efficient exploration of the hyperparameter space, reducing the computational burden associated with grid search.

The main advantage of randomized search is its ability to cover a wider range of hyperparameter values in a shorter amount of time. By sampling from a distribution, the search algorithm can discover unexpected combinations of hyperparameters that might yield better results than those explored in grid search. This flexibility makes randomized search particularly useful in situations where the optimal hyperparameters are unknown or hard to define.

The process of randomized search involves setting up a search space for each hyperparameter, specifying the distribution from which values will be randomly drawn. This distribution can be uniform, normal, or any other suitable distribution depending on the nature of the hyperparameter. The search algorithm then randomly samples values from each distribution, evaluates the model's performance using these hyperparameters, and keeps track of the best-performing configuration.

Randomized search is not only efficient but also robust to noise and less sensitive to small changes in hyperparameter values. It allows for a more exploratory approach to hyperparameter tuning, encouraging researchers and practitioners to think outside the box and experiment with different settings.

In conclusion, randomized search is a valuable tool in the arsenal of statistical modeling and machine learning practitioners. By providing a more efficient and flexible approach to hyperparameter tuning, it empowers researchers to explore a wider range of possibilities and ultimately improve the performance of their models. Whether you are a beginner or an experienced statistician, randomized search is a technique worth considering in your quest for optimal hyperparameters.

Bayesian Optimization

In the world of statistical modeling, there exists a powerful technique known as Bayesian Optimization. This approach combines the principles of Bayesian inference with optimization algorithms to efficiently find the optimal solution in complex and high-dimensional spaces. Whether you are a beginner or an expert in statistical modeling, Bayesian Optimization is a tool that can benefit everyone.

At its core, Bayesian Optimization is a sequential model-based optimization (SMBO) method that aims to find the best set of parameters for a given objective function. It works by iteratively proposing new candidate solutions, evaluating their performance, and updating a probabilistic model that represents the underlying function. By using Bayesian inference, this method incorporates prior knowledge and uncertainty into the optimization process, making it robust and adaptable to various scenarios.

One of the key advantages of Bayesian Optimization is its ability to handle expensive objective functions. In many real-world problems, evaluating the objective function can be time-consuming or resource-intensive. Bayesian Optimization addresses this challenge by intelligently selecting the next candidate solution based on the information gathered so far. By actively exploring promising regions and exploiting known good areas, it efficiently navigates the search space and converges to the optimal solution.

Another important aspect of Bayesian Optimization is the incorporation of prior beliefs. By specifying prior distributions over the parameters, users can inject their domain knowledge and biases into the optimization process. This is particularly valuable in situations where data is scarce or noisy, as the prior information helps guide the search towards more plausible regions and prevents overfitting.

Bayesian Optimization has found applications in various domains, including hyperparameter tuning for machine learning algorithms, experimental design in engineering, and drug discovery in pharmaceutical research. Its versatility and effectiveness make it a valuable tool for statisticians, data scientists, and researchers alike.

In this subchapter, we will explore the theoretical foundations of Bayesian Optimization, discuss different optimization algorithms commonly used in conjunction with this approach, and provide practical examples and case studies to illustrate its applications. By the end of this chapter, you will have a deep understanding of Bayesian Optimization and how it can be leveraged to solve complex statistical modeling problems. So whether you are a novice or an experienced practitioner, get ready to demystify Bayesian Optimization and unlock its potential in your statistical modeling endeavors.

Ensembling Techniques

Ensembling techniques are a powerful tool in the field of statistical modeling, offering a way to improve the accuracy and robustness of machine learning models. This subchapter will introduce you to the concept of ensembling and provide an overview of some popular ensembling techniques.

Ensembling refers to the process of combining multiple models to make predictions. The idea behind ensembling is that different models may have different strengths and weaknesses, and by combining their predictions, we can create a more reliable and accurate final prediction. Ensembling leverages the concept of the wisdom of the crowd, where diverse perspectives can lead to better outcomes.

One popular ensembling technique is called bagging, which stands for bootstrap aggregating. Bagging involves creating multiple variations of a base model by training each one on a different subset of the training data. The final prediction is then made by aggregating the predictions from each individual model, usually through majority voting or averaging. Bagging helps to reduce overfitting and increase stability by reducing the impact of individual noisy data points.

Another widely used ensembling technique is called boosting. Boosting works by training multiple weak models sequentially, with each subsequent model focusing on correcting the mistakes made by the previous models. Boosting assigns higher weights to misclassified data points, forcing subsequent models to pay more attention to these challenging instances. The final prediction is made by combining the predictions of all the weak models, typically using weighted voting.

Random forests are an extension of the bagging technique, where instead of using a single model as the base model, a forest of decision trees is used. Each tree is trained on a different subset of the training data and with a random subset of features. Random forests are known for their robustness, scalability, and resistance to overfitting, making them a popular choice for many machine learning tasks.

Stacking is another powerful ensembling technique that involves training multiple models and then using another model, called a meta-model, to combine their predictions. The meta-model is trained on the predictions made by the individual models, effectively learning to weigh their predictions based on their performance. Stacking allows for more complex and flexible combinations of models, often leading to improved performance.

Ensembling techniques have proven to be highly effective in improving the accuracy and reliability of machine learning models. By combining the strengths of different models, ensembling can help overcome the limitations and biases of individual models, leading to more robust predictions. Whether you are a beginner or an experienced practitioner in statistical modeling, understanding and applying ensembling techniques can take your machine learning skills to the next level. In the next sections, we will delve deeper into each ensembling technique and provide practical examples to help you implement them in your own projects.

Chapter 9: Handling Imbalanced Data and Bias

Understanding Imbalanced Data

In the world of statistical modeling and machine learning, dealing with imbalanced data is a common challenge that researchers and practitioners face. Imbalanced data refers to a situation where the classes or categories of interest are not equally represented in the dataset. This imbalance can lead to biased models and inaccurate predictions, making it crucial to understand and address this issue.

Imbalanced data occurs in various domains, such as fraud detection, medical diagnosis, and rare event prediction, where the occurrence of one class is significantly lower than the other(s). For example, in fraud detection, fraudulent transactions are relatively rare compared to legitimate ones. Similarly, in medical diagnosis, rare diseases may have limited instances compared to common ailments. Such imbalances can hinder the learning process of machine learning algorithms, as they tend to favor the majority class.

The effects of imbalanced data can be severe. Models trained on imbalanced data often struggle to predict the minority class accurately, leading to high false negatives. This is particularly problematic when dealing with critical situations such as detecting rare diseases or anomalies. Additionally, imbalanced data can result in overly optimistic performance metrics, as a model that simply predicts the majority class will still achieve high accuracy due to the unequal class distribution.

To overcome the challenges posed by imbalanced data, several techniques and strategies can be employed. One commonly used approach is resampling the dataset, which involves either oversampling the minority class or undersampling the majority class. Oversampling techniques include duplicating instances of the minority class or generating synthetic examples using algorithms like SMOTE (Synthetic Minority Over-sampling Technique). Undersampling, on the other hand, involves randomly removing instances from the majority class to balance the distribution.

Another approach is to modify the learning algorithms to give more weight or importance to the minority class. This can be achieved through techniques like cost-sensitive learning or adjusting class weights. By assigning higher penalties or costs to misclassifying the minority class, the algorithms can be trained to pay more attention to the underrepresented class.

Furthermore, ensemble methods such as bagging and boosting can also be effective in handling imbalanced data. These methods involve constructing multiple models and combining their predictions to achieve better performance. By training different models on different subsets of the imbalanced data, ensemble methods can help alleviate the bias towards the majority class.

In conclusion, understanding imbalanced data is vital for anyone involved in statistical modeling and machine learning. Recognizing the challenges it poses and employing appropriate techniques to tackle this issue is crucial for developing accurate and reliable models. By addressing the imbalance, we can ensure that our models are robust, unbiased, and capable of making sound predictions across all classes.

Techniques for Handling Imbalanced Data

Imbalanced data is a common problem in statistical modeling, where the number of observations belonging to one class is significantly higher than the other. This imbalance can lead to biased models that perform poorly in predicting the minority class. In this subchapter, we will explore various techniques for effectively handling imbalanced data in statistical modeling.

1. Resampling Techniques: Resampling techniques involve manipulating the dataset to balance the class distribution. Undersampling randomly removes instances from the majority class, while oversampling duplicates or generates synthetic instances for the minority class. Both approaches aim to create a balanced dataset for training the model.

2. Class Weighting: Class weighting assigns different weights to each class during the model training phase. Higher weights are typically assigned to the minority class, allowing the model to focus more on correctly classifying these instances. Class weighting can be incorporated into various algorithms, such as decision trees and support vector machines.

3. Ensemble Methods: Ensemble methods combine multiple models to improve the overall predictive performance. These methods can be particularly effective in handling imbalanced data by leveraging the strengths of different models. Techniques such as bagging, boosting, and stacking can be

used to create diverse models that collectively provide more accurate predictions.

4.   Cost-Sensitive   Learning: Cost-sensitive learning involves assigning different costs or penalties for misclassifying instances from different classes. This approach encourages the model to prioritize correctly classifying the minority class by penalizing misclassifications more heavily. By incorporating the costs of misclassification, the model can learn to make more informed decisions.

5.   Data   Augmentation: Data augmentation involves creating new synthetic instances by applying various transformations to the existing data. This technique can help in increasing the representation of the minority class by generating additional instances with similar characteristics. Techniques such as SMOTE (Synthetic Minority Over-sampling Technique) are commonly used for data augmentation.

It is important to note that the choice of technique for handling imbalanced data depends on the specific problem and dataset. It is recommended to experiment with multiple techniques to find the most suitable approach for a given situation. By effectively addressing the challenges posed by imbalanced data, statistical modeling can provide more accurate and unbiased predictions for a wide range of applications.

In conclusion, this subchapter has introduced several techniques for handling imbalanced data in statistical modeling. These techniques, including resampling, class weighting, ensemble methods, cost-sensitive learning, and data augmentation, can help improve the performance of models when dealing with imbalanced class distributions. By incorporating these techniques, statisticians and data scientists can ensure more robust and reliable predictions, contributing to the advancement of statistical modeling in various domains.

Addressing Bias in Machine Learning Models

Machine learning has become an integral part of our lives, shaping the way we make decisions and interact with technology. From personalized recommendations to autonomous vehicles, statistical modeling has revolutionized various industries. However, it is crucial to acknowledge that machine learning models are not immune to biases, which can lead to unfair and discriminatory outcomes. In this subchapter, we will delve into the importance of addressing bias in machine learning models and explore strategies to mitigate its impact.

Bias in machine learning models refers to the systematic errors that occur when the models favor certain groups or individuals over others. This bias can arise from various sources, including biased training data, biased feature selection, or even biased algorithm design. While unintentional, these biases can perpetuate societal inequalities and negatively impact marginalized communities.

To address bias in machine learning models, it is essential to adopt a proactive approach. Firstly, it is crucial to ensure that the training data used to develop the models is representative and diverse. By including data from various demographics and backgrounds, we can reduce the risk of biased outcomes. Additionally, data preprocessing techniques, such as data augmentation and oversampling, can be employed to balance the representation of different groups within the dataset.

Feature selection also plays a significant role in mitigating bias. It is important to carefully select features that are relevant and fair, avoiding those that might introduce or amplify biases. Regular monitoring and evaluation of model performance can help identify and rectify any biased outcomes. By examining the predictions and outcomes across different groups, we can detect and address any discrepancies or disparities.

Furthermore, algorithmic transparency and interpretability can aid in addressing bias. It is crucial to understand how the models make decisions and identify any underlying biases. By using interpretable models or techniques like model-agnostic interpretability, we can gain insights into the factors that contribute to biased outcomes and take corrective measures.

Lastly, it is essential to involve diverse stakeholders in the model development and evaluation process. By including individuals from different backgrounds and perspectives, we can gain a holistic understanding of potential biases and work towards creating more fair and equitable models.

Addressing bias in machine learning models is a collective responsibility. As practitioners of statistical modeling, it is imperative that we strive for fairness and inclusivity in our models. By being aware of the potential biases and adopting proactive strategies to mitigate them, we can contribute to the development of more reliable and trustworthy machine learning systems that benefit everyone.

In conclusion, addressing bias in machine learning models is a critical step towards creating equitable and fair systems. By considering diverse training data, careful feature selection, algorithmic transparency, and stakeholder involvement, we can work towards reducing biases and ensuring that statistical modeling benefits all individuals and communities.

Chapter 10: Real-World Applications of Machine Learning

Natural Language Processing

Natural Language Processing (NLP) is a fascinating subfield of artificial intelligence that focuses on enabling computers to understand, interpret, and generate human language. In today's digital age, where we are surrounded by an ever-growing amount of text data, NLP plays a crucial role in analyzing, extracting meaning, and deriving insights from this vast information.

NLP techniques have revolutionized the way we interact with computers and have become an integral part of our daily lives. From virtual assistants like Siri and Alexa to language translation services and sentiment analysis tools, NLP has permeated various domains, making machines more intelligent and capable of understanding human language.

At its core, NLP combines principles from computer science, linguistics, and statistics to process and analyze human language. Statistical modeling, a powerful tool in the field of data analysis, is particularly important in NLP. By applying statistical techniques, NLP algorithms learn patterns and structures in language data, enabling them to perform tasks such as text classification, named entity recognition, sentiment analysis, and machine translation.

This subchapter aims to demystify NLP and provide an introductory understanding of its principles and applications. It will delve into various statistical modeling techniques employed in NLP, explaining how these models process and interpret natural language. From the basics of tokenization and stemming to more advanced techniques like language modeling and word embeddings, this subchapter will cover a broad range of topics to equip readers with a holistic understanding of NLP.

Moreover, this subchapter will also explore the challenges and limitations associated with NLP. Despite significant advancements, machines still struggle with understanding context, ambiguity, and nuances in language, making NLP a challenging field. By understanding the limitations of NLP, readers will gain a realistic perspective on what can and cannot be achieved using current techniques.

Whether you are a data scientist, a linguist, or simply curious about the world of NLP, this subchapter will provide you with a solid foundation to explore further. By demystifying the complexities of NLP and statistical modeling, this subchapter aims to make the seemingly intimidating field accessible to everyone interested in leveraging the power of natural language for better data analysis and decision making.

Computer Vision

Computer vision is a fascinating field within the realm of machine learning and statistical modeling. It is the technology that allows computers to understand and interpret visual information from the real world, just like humans do. By harnessing the power of statistical modeling, computer vision has the potential to revolutionize various industries and improve our daily lives.

In this subchapter, we will demystify computer vision and explore its applications, algorithms, and techniques. Whether you are a beginner or an expert in statistical modeling, this section will provide you with a comprehensive overview of computer vision and its significance in today's world.

Firstly, we will delve into the basics of computer vision, discussing the fundamental concepts and terminologies used in this field. We will explore how computers are capable of perceiving and understanding images and videos, and how statistical modeling plays a crucial role in this process. By grasping these foundations, you will be better equipped to comprehend the more complex topics ahead.

Next, we will dive into the different algorithms and techniques used in computer vision. We will explore image processing, object detection, image recognition, and image segmentation, among other topics. By understanding these algorithms, you will gain insights into how computers can identify objects, recognize faces, and extract meaningful information from images and videos.

Furthermore, we will discuss the practical applications of computer vision across various industries. From healthcare and autonomous vehicles to security systems and augmented reality, computer vision has the potential to transform the way we interact with technology and the world around us. We will explore real-world examples and case studies to illustrate how statistical modeling is being leveraged to solve complex problems and drive innovation.

Lastly, we will touch upon the challenges and future directions of computer vision. We will discuss the limitations of current algorithms, ethical considerations, and potential areas of improvement. As computer vision continues to evolve, statistical modeling will play a vital role in pushing the boundaries and unlocking new possibilities.

Whether you are a data scientist, a software developer, or simply curious about the fascinating world of statistical modeling, this subchapter on computer vision will provide you with a comprehensive understanding of this exciting field. By demystifying computer vision, we aim to empower everyone to explore and contribute to the advancements in this transformative technology.

Recommender Systems

In today's fast-paced world, we are constantly bombarded with an overwhelming amount of information and choices. Whether it's choosing a movie to watch, a book to read, or a product to buy, the sheer number of options can be paralyzing. This is where recommender systems come to the rescue.

Recommender systems are powerful tools that help us navigate this information overload by providing personalized recommendations tailored to our specific interests and preferences. These systems are built on statistical modeling techniques and have revolutionized the way we discover new content.

At its core, a recommender system analyzes a vast amount of data, ranging from user preferences and historical behavior to item characteristics and similarities. By leveraging advanced statistical modeling algorithms, these systems can make accurate predictions about what users are likely to enjoy or find useful.

There are two main types of recommender systems: content-based and collaborative filtering. Content-based recommender systems analyze the characteristics of items that a user has liked or interacted with in the past and recommend similar items. For example, if a user has shown an interest in action movies, the system might suggest other action-packed films.

On the other hand, collaborative filtering recommender systems rely on the collective intelligence of a large user base. They analyze patterns of behavior and preferences across a group of users to generate recommendations. For instance, if many users who have similar tastes to mine have rated a particular book highly, the system might recommend it to me as well.

One of the key challenges in building recommender systems is the so-called "cold start" problem. This refers to situations where there is limited or no data available for new users or items. To overcome this challenge, hybrid recommender systems combine multiple approaches, such as content-based and collaborative filtering, to provide accurate recommendations even in the absence of sufficient data.

Recommender systems have become an integral part of our daily lives, improving the way we consume content and make decisions. From personalized movie recommendations on streaming platforms to product suggestions on e-commerce websites, these systems have transformed the way we discover and engage with information.

In this book, "Demystifying Machine Learning: A Statistical Modeling Guide for Everyone," we will delve into the intricacies of building effective recommender systems. From understanding the underlying statistical modeling techniques to implementing and evaluating these systems, this subchapter will equip you with the knowledge and skills needed to develop your own recommender systems. So whether you are a data scientist, a business analyst, or simply someone interested in statistical modeling, this chapter is for you. Let's demystify recommender systems together and unlock the power of personalized recommendations.

Fraud Detection

Fraud is a pervasive problem that affects a wide range of industries and has significant financial implications. As technology advances, so do the methods used by fraudsters to deceive businesses and individuals. In today's world, it is becoming increasingly challenging to manually identify and prevent fraudulent activities. This is where the power of statistical modeling and machine learning comes into play.

In this subchapter, we will explore the fascinating world of fraud detection through the lens of statistical modeling. Whether you are a business owner, a data scientist, or simply someone interested in understanding how fraud detection works, this chapter will provide you with valuable insights.

To begin, we will define fraud and its various forms. From credit card fraud to insurance fraud, we will delve into the different types of fraudulent activities that plague our society. Understanding the nuances of fraud is essential for developing effective detection models.

Next, we will explore the statistical modeling techniques commonly used for fraud detection. From logistic regression to decision trees and random forests, we will discuss the strengths and weaknesses of each method. We will also touch upon anomaly detection techniques, which are particularly useful when dealing with new, previously unseen types of fraud.

One crucial aspect of fraud detection is feature engineering. We will guide you through the process of selecting and engineering meaningful features that can help distinguish between legitimate and fraudulent transactions. You will learn about feature selection techniques, outlier detection, and the importance of domain knowledge in building accurate fraud detection models.

We will also address the challenges and limitations of fraud detection using statistical modeling. Fraudsters are constantly evolving their tactics, and our models must be able to adapt and learn from new patterns. We will discuss strategies for model monitoring, updating, and fine-tuning to ensure continued effectiveness in fraud prevention.

Lastly, we will provide practical examples and case studies that demonstrate the real-world applications of statistical modeling in fraud detection. These examples will showcase how statistical modeling can be leveraged to identify fraudulent activities, save businesses from financial losses, and protect individuals from falling victim to scams.

By the end of this subchapter, you will have a solid understanding of how statistical modeling can help combat fraud. Whether you are a business professional looking to implement fraud detection systems or a data enthusiast interested in the intricacies of statistical modeling, this subchapter will equip you with the knowledge you need to make a difference in the fight against fraud.

Remember, fraud affects us all, and it is through knowledge, awareness, and the power of statistical modeling that we can stay one step ahead of the fraudsters.

Healthcare Applications

Machine learning has found extensive applications in the healthcare industry, revolutionizing the way medical practitioners diagnose, treat, and manage diseases. The integration of statistical modeling techniques with machine learning algorithms has paved the way for more accurate predictions, personalized medicine, and improved patient outcomes. In this subchapter, we will explore some of the remarkable healthcare applications of machine learning and statistical modeling.

One of the key areas where machine learning has made significant advancements is in medical imaging. With the help of deep learning algorithms, radiologists can now detect and diagnose various diseases from X-rays, MRI scans, and CT scans with remarkable accuracy. Machine learning models can analyze vast amounts of medical images, identify patterns, and assist radiologists in detecting conditions such as tumors, fractures, and abnormalities in a fraction of the time it would take a human expert.

Another critical application of machine learning in healthcare is predictive modeling for early disease detection. By leveraging patient data, such as electronic health records, lab results, and genetic information, statistical models can be built to identify individuals at high risk of developing certain conditions like diabetes, cardiovascular diseases, or cancer. These models help healthcare providers intervene at an early stage, potentially preventing the progression of the disease and improving patient outcomes.

Machine learning algorithms also play a crucial role in drug discovery and development. By analyzing vast amounts of molecular data, including chemical structures and biological interactions, models can predict the efficacy and potential side effects of new drugs. This accelerates the drug discovery process and reduces the cost and time associated with bringing new treatments to market.

Furthermore, machine learning has enabled the development of personalized medicine, tailoring treatments and interventions to individual patients. By considering a patient's genetic makeup, medical history, lifestyle factors, and response to previous treatments, statistical models can assist in determining the most effective treatment plan for each patient. This approach not only improves patient outcomes but also reduces the risk of adverse reactions and unnecessary treatments.

In conclusion, the integration of statistical modeling and machine learning has brought significant advancements to the healthcare industry. From improving diagnostic accuracy to enabling personalized medicine, these technologies hold immense potential to transform patient care. As machine learning continues to evolve, it is imperative for healthcare professionals to understand and embrace these tools to provide the best possible care for all patients. Whether you are a medical practitioner, researcher, or simply interested in the field of statistical modeling, this subchapter will provide valuable insights into the healthcare applications of machine learning.

Chapter 11: Ethical Considerations in Machine Learning

Bias and Fairness in Machine Learning

In the rapidly evolving field of machine learning, it is crucial to address the important concepts of bias and fairness. As machine learning algorithms continue to make decisions that impact our lives, it is essential that these decisions are fair and unbiased. This subchapter aims to demystify the topic of bias and fairness in machine learning, providing a comprehensive understanding for everyone, particularly those interested in statistical modeling.

Bias in machine learning refers to a systematic error that is introduced during the learning process. This bias occurs when the algorithm consistently predicts certain outcomes more accurately than others. It can arise from various sources, such as biased training data, biased features, or biased assumptions in the algorithm itself. Understanding and mitigating bias is crucial for ensuring the fairness and ethicality of machine learning systems.

Fairness, on the other hand, pertains to the equitable treatment of individuals or groups. In the context of machine learning, fairness means that the algorithm's predictions and decisions should not be influenced by irrelevant factors such as race, gender, or socio-economic background. Achieving fairness in machine learning is challenging due to the inherent biases present in the data and the potential for biased decision-making by the algorithm.

This subchapter will delve into various aspects of bias and fairness in machine learning. It will discuss the different types of bias, including selection bias, measurement bias, and confirmation bias, and how they can impact the outcomes of machine learning algorithms. The subchapter will also explore the ethical implications of biased algorithms and the potential consequences for individuals and society as a whole.

Furthermore, the subchapter will present various techniques and approaches to mitigate bias and promote fairness in machine learning. These may include pre-processing techniques like data augmentation and sampling, as well as post-processing techniques like reweighing and calibration. The subchapter will also emphasize the importance of transparency and interpretability in machine learning models, as these factors play a crucial role in understanding and addressing bias.

By the end of this subchapter, readers will have a comprehensive understanding of the challenges posed by bias and fairness in machine learning. They will be equipped with the knowledge and tools necessary to recognize and mitigate bias in their own statistical modeling endeavors. Whether you are a beginner in the field of statistical modeling or an expert seeking to improve your machine learning algorithms, this subchapter will provide valuable insights and practical guidance for ensuring fairness and ethicality in your models.

Privacy and Data Protection

In today's digital age, where information is constantly being shared and collected, the issue of privacy and data protection has become more crucial than ever before. As statistical modeling plays a significant role in analyzing and interpreting data, it is essential for everyone, regardless of their background, to understand the importance of safeguarding personal information.

The subchapter "Privacy and Data Protection" aims to demystify the complexities surrounding this topic and provide a comprehensive guide for individuals interested in statistical modeling. Whether you are an experienced data scientist or a curious enthusiast, this subchapter will equip you with the knowledge and tools needed to navigate the intricate landscape of privacy and data protection.

The subchapter begins by defining the fundamental concepts of privacy and data protection in the context of statistical modeling. It explores the various types of data that are commonly used in statistical modeling and delves into the potential risks associated with their collection and usage. By understanding these risks, readers will gain a heightened awareness of the importance of protecting personal data.

Next, the subchapter explores different methods and techniques for ensuring privacy and data protection in statistical modeling. It covers topics such as anonymization, pseudonymization, and encryption, explaining how these methods can be employed to prevent unauthorized access and protect sensitive information. Furthermore, it discusses the legal and ethical considerations surrounding data protection, shedding light on the regulations and guidelines that govern the collection and usage of personal data.

To provide a practical understanding of these concepts, real-world examples and case studies are included throughout the subchapter. These examples demonstrate the potential consequences of inadequate privacy measures and highlight the impact of data breaches on individuals and organizations. By examining these cases, readers will gain a deeper understanding of the importance of privacy and data protection in statistical modeling.

In conclusion, "Privacy and Data Protection" is a vital subchapter within the book "Demystifying Machine Learning: A Statistical Modeling Guide for Everyone." It serves as a comprehensive resource for individuals interested in statistical modeling and provides the necessary knowledge and tools to protect personal information. By understanding the risks, methods, and legal considerations associated with data protection, readers will be able to navigate the world of statistical modeling with confidence and ensure the ethical and responsible use of data in their work.

Transparency and Accountability

In the realm of statistical modeling, transparency and accountability are crucial elements that must be upheld to ensure the integrity and effectiveness of machine learning algorithms. This subchapter aims to shed light on the significance of transparency and accountability in statistical modeling, emphasizing their relevance to everyone, regardless of their expertise in the field.

Transparency refers to the ability to understand and interpret the decision-making process of machine learning models. It is essential for researchers, practitioners, and individuals affected by these models to have access to information about how the algorithms arrive at their predictions or recommendations. Transparent models allow for better scrutiny, evaluation, and identification of potential biases or errors that may influence the outcomes. By promoting transparency, we can enhance trust in statistical models and foster a deeper understanding of the underlying mechanisms.

Accountability goes hand in hand with transparency, as it focuses on the responsibility and consequences associated with the use of machine learning models. It is crucial to acknowledge that statistical models can have far-reaching implications in various domains, including healthcare, finance, criminal justice, and more. Therefore, it is essential to hold individuals and organizations accountable for the decisions made based on these models. This requires establishing clear guidelines, ethical frameworks, and regulations that promote fairness, privacy, and non-discrimination.

For statistical modeling to be truly inclusive and beneficial for everyone, it is important to address the potential biases and limitations inherent in these algorithms. Machine learning models, despite their power and accuracy, are not infallible. They can inadvertently perpetuate biases present in the data used for training, leading to unfair outcomes and discrimination. By acknowledging these biases and actively working to mitigate them, we can strive for more equitable and unbiased statistical modeling.

To achieve transparency and accountability, various approaches can be employed. These include model documentation, providing explanations for predictions, and third-party audits to verify the fairness and accuracy of the models. Additionally, involving diverse stakeholders in the development and evaluation of statistical models can help ensure a broader perspective and reduce the risk of unintended consequences.

Regardless of one's expertise in statistical modeling, it is crucial to be aware of the principles of transparency and accountability. As individuals, we can demand transparency from the organizations and institutions that utilize machine learning models. By advocating for fairness, ethical practices, and accountability, we can contribute to a more inclusive and responsible application of statistical modeling techniques.

In conclusion, transparency and accountability are vital components of statistical modeling. They enable us to understand the decision-making process of machine learning algorithms, identify potential biases, and hold individuals and organizations responsible for the outcomes. By championing transparency and accountability, we can promote fairness, reduce discrimination, and ensure that statistical modeling benefits everyone.

Chapter 12: Case Studies and Practical Examples

Predicting Housing Prices

In today's fast-paced real estate market, accurately predicting housing prices has become a critical task for buyers, sellers, and investors alike. With the advancements in statistical modeling and the emergence of machine learning techniques, we now have powerful tools at our disposal to make informed decisions about property values. This subchapter aims to demystify the process of predicting housing prices, making it accessible to everyone with an interest in statistical modeling.

Before delving into the techniques used for predicting housing prices, it is important to understand the relevance and impact of statistical modeling in this domain. Statistical modeling involves analyzing historical data to uncover patterns and relationships between variables. By applying these patterns to new data, we can make predictions with a certain level of confidence. This approach is particularly beneficial in the real estate industry, where factors such as location, size, amenities, and market trends can greatly influence property value.

One of the most popular techniques used for predicting housing prices is multiple linear regression. This method involves identifying a set of independent variables, such as the number of bedrooms, square footage, and location, that are statistically significant predictors of the dependent variable, i.e., the housing price. By fitting a linear equation to the data, we can estimate the impact of each independent variable on the housing price.

Another powerful tool is decision trees, which can handle both categorical and numerical variables. Decision trees split the data based on different attributes and create branches to reach a prediction. This approach allows us to capture nonlinear relationships and interactions between variables, resulting in more accurate predictions.

In recent years, machine learning algorithms such as random forests and gradient boosting have gained popularity for predicting housing prices. These algorithms combine multiple decision trees to create a robust model that can handle complex data patterns and outliers. They also offer feature importance analysis, enabling us to identify the variables that have the most significant impact on housing prices.

Furthermore, advancements in deep learning have introduced neural networks as a promising method for predicting housing prices. Neural networks are composed of interconnected nodes that mimic the structure and functioning of the human brain. By training these networks on large datasets, they can learn complex patterns and relationships, leading to accurate predictions.

In conclusion, predicting housing prices is an essential task in the real estate industry. By utilizing statistical modeling techniques, we can harness the power of historical data to make informed decisions about property values. Whether you are a buyer, seller, or investor, understanding these techniques will empower you to navigate the real estate market with confidence.

Customer Churn Prediction

In today's highly competitive business landscape, customer churn has become a critical concern for companies across various industries. The ability to accurately predict which customers are likely to churn is of utmost importance as it enables businesses to take proactive measures to retain valuable customers and minimize revenue loss. This subchapter, "Customer Churn Prediction," delves into the realm of statistical modeling and provides valuable insights into how machine learning techniques can be leveraged to predict customer churn.

Addressed to everyone, from beginners to experienced professionals in statistical modeling, this subchapter aims to demystify the complex world of machine learning and make it accessible to all. Even if you have no prior knowledge of statistical modeling or machine learning, this chapter will provide you with a solid foundation to understand and apply these techniques effectively.

The subchapter begins by introducing the concept of customer churn and its significance in driving business success. It explains how customer churn impacts a company's bottom line and emphasizes the need for proactive measures to identify and mitigate this issue. It then delves into the various statistical modeling techniques used for customer churn prediction, such as logistic regression, decision trees, random forests, and support vector machines.

The chapter also provides a step-by-step guide on how to build a customer churn prediction model using machine learning. It covers essential topics like data preprocessing, feature engineering, model selection, and evaluation metrics. The aim is to equip the audience with practical knowledge that they can apply to their own business problems.

Furthermore, the subchapter highlights the challenges and limitations associated with customer churn prediction. It emphasizes the importance of continuous monitoring and model updating to ensure the accuracy and relevance of predictions over time.

Through real-world examples and case studies, this subchapter demonstrates how statistical modeling can be leveraged to predict customer churn effectively. It also discusses the ethical considerations involved in using customer data and provides guidelines for responsible and ethical data handling.

Overall, "Customer Churn Prediction" is an essential subchapter for anyone interested in understanding and applying statistical modeling techniques to predict customer churn. By demystifying machine learning concepts and offering practical guidance, it empowers individuals from all backgrounds to harness the power of data-driven insights and make informed decisions to drive business success.

Sentiment Analysis

In today's digital age, where opinions and emotions are expressed freely on various online platforms, understanding the sentiment behind these expressions has become increasingly important. This is where sentiment analysis, a powerful application of statistical modeling, comes into play. In this subchapter, we will demystify sentiment analysis and explore its significance in understanding and interpreting human emotions.

Sentiment analysis, also known as opinion mining, is the process of using statistical modeling techniques to determine the sentiment, attitude, or emotions conveyed in a given text. It involves analyzing the words, phrases, and context to classify the sentiment as positive, negative, or neutral. By harnessing the power of machine learning algorithms, sentiment analysis enables us to extract meaningful insights from vast amounts of unstructured text data.

The applications of sentiment analysis are vast and diverse. In the business world, sentiment analysis helps companies understand customer feedback, monitor brand reputation, and make data-driven decisions based on customer sentiment. It also plays a crucial role in market research, as it can provide valuable insights into consumer preferences, trends, and the overall sentiment towards products or services.

Beyond business applications, sentiment analysis has proven to be an invaluable tool in social media monitoring, political analysis, and even healthcare. By analyzing social media posts, sentiment analysis can help identify emerging trends, gauge public opinion, and measure the sentiment towards a particular topic or event. In politics, sentiment analysis can provide insights into public sentiment towards political candidates or policies, aiding campaign strategies and policy-making decisions.

Now, you might wonder, how does sentiment analysis actually work? Well, it utilizes a combination of machine learning algorithms, natural language processing techniques, and linguistic rules. Initially, a sentiment analysis model is trained on a labeled dataset, where human annotators assign sentiments to a set of texts. The model then learns patterns and associations between words and sentiments, allowing it to predict sentiment labels on unseen data.

However, sentiment analysis is not without challenges. Contextual understanding, sarcasm, and language nuances can complicate sentiment classification. To overcome these challenges, advanced techniques like sentiment lexicons, deep learning models, and ensemble methods are used to improve the accuracy and robustness of sentiment analysis systems.

In conclusion, sentiment analysis is a powerful tool in the field of statistical modeling that helps us unravel the emotions and opinions hidden within texts. Its applications are vast and diverse, making it relevant to everyone, from businesses seeking customer insights to researchers analyzing social trends. By understanding sentiment analysis, we unlock the potential to make data-driven decisions and gain deeper insights into human emotions in an increasingly digital world.

Credit Risk Assessment

Credit risk assessment is a crucial aspect of financial modeling and decision-making. In this subchapter, we will delve into the fundamentals of credit risk assessment, its significance in statistical modeling, and its relevance to everyone, regardless of their background or expertise.

Credit risk assessment involves evaluating the potential of a borrower defaulting on their loan or credit obligations. This assessment is essential for lenders, banks, and financial institutions to make informed decisions about extending credit to individuals or businesses. By utilizing statistical modeling techniques, lenders can assess the creditworthiness of borrowers and determine the likelihood of default.

Statistical modeling plays a pivotal role in credit risk assessment. It enables lenders to analyze historical data, identify patterns, and build predictive models that quantify the risk associated with lending. By incorporating various factors such as income, employment history, credit history, and other relevant variables, statistical models can generate credit scores or ratings that provide a measure of the borrower's creditworthiness.

Understanding credit risk assessment is essential for everyone, not just professionals in the field of statistical modeling. Whether you are a borrower seeking credit, a small business owner, or an investor, comprehending the basics of credit risk assessment empowers you to make informed financial decisions. It allows you to evaluate the risks involved in borrowing or investing, negotiate better loan terms, or assess the stability of potential business partners.

Moreover, credit risk assessment is crucial for individuals looking to improve their creditworthiness. By understanding the factors that contribute to a credit score, individuals can take proactive measures to enhance their financial standing. This may include paying bills on time, reducing outstanding debt, or maintaining a stable employment record.

In this subchapter, we will cover various statistical modeling techniques commonly used in credit risk assessment, such as logistic regression, decision trees, or random forests. We will explain the concept of feature selection, discuss the importance of model validation, and highlight common pitfalls to avoid when building credit risk models.

By the end of this subchapter, you will have a solid understanding of credit risk assessment, its role in statistical modeling, and its relevance to your personal financial decisions. Whether you are a professional in the field or simply someone interested in improving their financial literacy, this subchapter will provide you with valuable insights into the world of credit risk assessment.

Image Classification

In the world of statistical modeling, image classification is a fascinating and powerful technique that has gained significant popularity in recent years. This subchapter will demystify the concepts and techniques behind image classification and provide a comprehensive understanding of its applications in various fields.

Image classification is the process of categorizing images into predefined classes or labels based on their visual content. The goal is to enable machines to automatically recognize and differentiate between different objects or patterns within images. This technique has found widespread applications in areas like healthcare, self-driving cars, facial recognition, satellite imagery analysis, and much more.

At its core, image classification involves training a machine learning model with a labeled dataset. The model learns to recognize patterns and features in the images and assigns them to appropriate classes. Convolutional Neural Networks (CNNs) have emerged as the state-of-the-art method for image classification due to their ability to capture complex spatial relationships within images.

To build a successful image classification model, several steps need to be followed. Firstly, the dataset must be collected and labeled appropriately, ensuring a diverse representation of each class. Preprocessing techniques such as resizing, normalization, and augmentation may be applied to enhance the dataset quality.

Next, the labeled dataset is split into training and testing sets. The training set is used to train the model, while the testing set is used to evaluate its performance on unseen data. It is crucial to use appropriate evaluation metrics such as accuracy, precision, recall, and F1-score to measure the model's performance accurately.

During training, the model learns to extract meaningful features from the images using convolutional layers and then makes predictions using fully connected layers. The process involves iteratively adjusting the model's weights and biases to minimize the difference between predicted and actual labels.

Regularization techniques, such as dropout and weight decay, are often employed to prevent overfitting, where the model becomes too specialized on the training data and fails to generalize well to new, unseen images.

Once the model is trained, it can be deployed to make predictions on new, unseen images. This process involves passing the image through the trained model and obtaining the predicted label. The model's performance can be further improved by fine-tuning on additional data or through techniques like transfer learning.

Image classification is revolutionizing various industries by enabling automated analysis of vast amounts of visual data. From medical diagnoses to autonomous vehicles, the ability to accurately classify images has become an essential tool for decision-making and problem-solving.

By understanding the concepts and techniques behind image classification, individuals from all backgrounds can harness the power of statistical modeling to develop innovative solutions and contribute to the advancements in this rapidly evolving field. Whether you are a healthcare professional, a computer science enthusiast, or simply curious about cutting-edge technologies, this subchapter will equip you with the knowledge needed to navigate the world of image classification.

Chapter 13: Future Trends in Machine Learning

Deep Learning and Neural Networks

In recent years, there has been an explosion of interest and excitement surrounding the field of machine learning. One of the most powerful and promising techniques in this field is deep learning, which is based on the concept of neural networks. Deep learning has revolutionized the way we approach complex problems and has achieved remarkable success in various domains such as computer vision, natural language processing, and speech recognition.

At its core, deep learning is a subset of machine learning that focuses on training artificial neural networks to mimic the human brain. These neural networks consist of interconnected layers of nodes, or artificial neurons, which process and transform data as it passes through the network. The depth of these networks refers to the number of layers they contain, hence the term "deep learning."

Neural networks are designed to learn from large amounts of labeled data, allowing them to recognize patterns, make predictions, and make decisions. By using a technique called backpropagation, neural networks can adjust their weights and biases to optimize their performance. This iterative process of training allows neural networks to improve their accuracy over time and adapt to new data.

Deep learning has proven to be particularly effective in handling complex and unstructured data, such as images, audio, and text. Convolutional neural networks (CNNs), a type of neural network commonly used in computer vision tasks, have achieved unprecedented accuracy in tasks like image classification and object detection. Recurrent neural networks (RNNs), on the other hand, excel in capturing sequential and temporal dependencies, making them ideal for tasks like speech recognition and machine translation.

While deep learning has shown great promise and achieved remarkable results, it is not without its challenges. Training deep neural networks requires vast amounts of labeled data and considerable computational resources. Furthermore, interpreting the inner workings of neural networks can be difficult due to their complex and often opaque nature.

Nonetheless, deep learning and neural networks have opened up new possibilities and opportunities in the field of statistical modeling. With the right tools and techniques, anyone can harness the power of deep learning to solve complex problems and make accurate predictions. Whether you are a beginner or an experienced practitioner, understanding deep learning and neural networks is essential for staying at the forefront of statistical modeling and machine learning.

In the following chapters, we will delve deeper into the concepts, techniques, and applications of deep learning. We will explore the different types of neural networks, discuss their training algorithms, and provide practical examples and case studies. By the end of this book, you will have gained a solid foundation in deep learning and be equipped with the knowledge and skills to apply it in your own statistical modeling endeavors.

Reinforcement Learning

Reinforcement Learning is a powerful concept in the field of machine learning that has garnered significant attention in recent years. It is a subfield of artificial intelligence that focuses on teaching machines to make decisions and take actions based on their environment. This subchapter aims to demystify Reinforcement Learning, making it accessible to everyone, particularly those interested in statistical modeling.

At its core, Reinforcement Learning is about teaching an agent how to interact with an environment to maximize a reward signal. Unlike supervised learning, where the agent is provided with labeled examples, or unsupervised learning, where the agent must find patterns in unlabeled data, reinforcement learning is based on trial and error. The agent learns through continuous interactions with the environment, receiving feedback in the form of rewards or penalties for its actions.

This subchapter will explore the fundamental concepts of Reinforcement Learning, starting with the key components: the agent, the environment, and the reward signal. It will delve into the concept of the Markov Decision Process (MDP), which provides a mathematical framework to model sequential decision-making problems. Through MDPs, the reader will gain an understanding of how the agent's actions impact its future states and rewards.

Next, various algorithms used in Reinforcement Learning will be discussed, such as Q-Learning and policy gradients. These algorithms enable the agent to learn optimal strategies and policies by exploring different actions and evaluating their long-term consequences. The subchapter will explain the intuition behind these algorithms and their mathematical foundations, while emphasizing their relevance to statistical modeling.

Furthermore, this subchapter will cover applications of Reinforcement Learning in a wide range of fields, including robotics, game playing, and autonomous driving. It will highlight the potential of this approach to solve complex problems where traditional statistical modeling techniques may fall short. Real-world examples and case studies will be provided to illustrate the practicality and effectiveness of Reinforcement Learning in various domains.

By the end of this subchapter, readers will have a solid understanding of the principles and applications of Reinforcement Learning in statistical modeling. They will be equipped with the knowledge to apply these concepts to their own projects and explore the vast potential of this exciting field. Whether you are a novice or an experienced practitioner, this subchapter will demystify Reinforcement Learning and empower you to harness its power in your own work.

Explainable AI

In recent years, the field of artificial intelligence (AI) has made tremendous strides, transforming various industries and revolutionizing the way we live and work. However, one significant challenge that arises from the increasing complexity of AI systems is their lack of transparency and explainability. This subchapter aims to shed light on the concept of Explainable AI (XAI) and its importance in the context of statistical modeling.

Explainable AI refers to the ability of AI systems to provide clear and understandable explanations for their decisions and actions. While traditional statistical modeling techniques often yield interpretable results, the rise of complex machine learning algorithms, such as deep neural networks, has made it challenging to understand how these models arrive at their predictions. This lack of interpretability has raised concerns regarding the ethical, legal, and societal implications of AI systems, particularly in high-stakes domains like healthcare, finance, and criminal justice.

The need for explainability stems from the desire to build trust and confidence in AI systems. By providing insights into the decision-making process, explainable AI enables users to understand why a particular prediction or outcome is produced. This transparency allows stakeholders to validate the model's behavior, identify potential biases, and detect any unintended consequences. Additionally, explainability facilitates regulatory compliance, as certain industries require justifiable and transparent decision-making processes.

Several techniques have been proposed to achieve explainability in AI systems. One approach is to use simpler, interpretable models, such as decision trees or linear regression, as proxies for more complex models. These surrogate models approximate the behavior of the black-box models, providing insights into their decision-making process. Another technique involves generating explanations alongside predictions, such as highlighting the most influential features or providing textual justifications for the model's output.

It is important to note that achieving explainability in AI systems is a multidisciplinary effort, involving statisticians, computer scientists, ethicists, and domain experts. While there is ongoing research in this area, striking a balance between model performance and interpretability remains a challenge. Moreover, trade-offs must be made between transparency and model complexity, as highly interpretable models may sacrifice predictive accuracy.

In conclusion, Explainable AI plays a critical role in addressing the opacity of complex machine learning models. By providing understandable explanations, stakeholders can trust AI systems, identify potential biases, and ensure compliance with regulations. As the field of statistical modeling continues to evolve, it is crucial to incorporate explainability into AI systems to unlock their full potential while maintaining transparency and accountability.

AutoML and Automated Machine Learning

In recent years, the field of machine learning has made tremendous advancements, and it is now being used in various industries to solve complex problems and make data-driven decisions. However, the implementation of machine learning models can be a daunting task for many, especially those without a strong background in statistical modeling. This is where AutoML and automated machine learning come into play.

AutoML, short for Automated Machine Learning, refers to the process of automating the various stages of building, training, and deploying machine learning models. It aims to make machine learning accessible to everyone, regardless of their statistical modeling expertise. AutoML tools and platforms simplify the entire machine learning pipeline, from data preprocessing to model evaluation, making it easier for even non-experts to leverage the power of machine learning.

Automated machine learning algorithms work by automatically searching and selecting the best model architecture and hyperparameters for a given dataset. They employ techniques such as neural architecture search, hyperparameter optimization, and feature engineering to streamline the model building process. This eliminates the need for manual trial and error, saving significant time and effort for users.

One of the key advantages of AutoML is its ability to democratize machine learning. By automating the complex aspects of model building, AutoML empowers individuals from various backgrounds to leverage machine learning in their work. This is particularly beneficial for those in the statistical modeling niche who may not have the time or resources to delve into the intricacies of machine learning algorithms.

Moreover, AutoML enables faster prototyping and experimentation. With automated machine learning, statistical modelers can quickly iterate through different models and hyperparameters, allowing them to explore a wider range of possibilities and improve the model's performance. This rapid experimentation helps in identifying the best approach for a given problem, leading to more accurate predictions and insights.

However, it is essential to note that while AutoML simplifies the model building process, it does not replace the need for domain expertise and human intervention. Automated machine learning tools should be seen as a facilitator rather than a complete solution. Understanding the underlying principles of statistical modeling and the nuances of the dataset is crucial to interpret and validate the results produced by the AutoML algorithms.

In conclusion, AutoML and automated machine learning have revolutionized the field of statistical modeling by making machine learning more accessible to everyone. These tools and platforms streamline the model building process, saving time and effort for non-experts. By automating complex tasks, AutoML allows statistical modelers to experiment more rapidly and explore a wider range of models and hyperparameters. However, human expertise and domain knowledge remain essential to interpret and validate the results generated by AutoML algorithms. With AutoML, even those with limited statistical modeling experience can harness the power of machine learning to make data-driven decisions and solve complex problems.

Chapter 14: Conclusion and Next Steps

Recap of Key Concepts

In this subchapter, we will recapitulate the key concepts discussed throughout the book "Demystifying Machine Learning: A Statistical Modeling Guide for Everyone." This recap aims to reinforce your understanding of statistical modeling and machine learning, making it more accessible and applicable to a wide range of audiences.

Statistical Modeling is a powerful tool used to analyze and interpret complex data sets. It involves the application of mathematical and statistical techniques to uncover patterns, relationships, and insights that can inform decision-making processes. Machine Learning, on the other hand, focuses on the development of algorithms and models that enable computers to learn from data and make predictions or decisions without explicit programming.

Throughout this book, we have explored essential concepts that form the foundation of statistical modeling and machine learning. We began by introducing the fundamental concepts of data, variables, and the importance of data preprocessing. We discussed the significance of understanding the data structure, identifying missing values, and dealing with outliers to ensure the reliability and accuracy of our models.

Next, we delved into the various types of statistical models, including linear regression, logistic regression, decision trees, and random forests. We explored how these models can be used for both regression and classification tasks, highlighting their strengths and limitations.

Additionally, we examined the importance of model evaluation and validation techniques such as cross-validation and ROC curves.

Feature selection and dimensionality reduction techniques were also covered in-depth. We discussed how to identify the most relevant features and reduce the number of variables to improve model performance and reduce computational complexity. Techniques like Principal Component Analysis (PCA) and Recursive Feature Elimination (RFE) were explored for this purpose.

Moreover, we addressed the challenges of overfitting and underfitting and discussed regularization techniques such as L1 and L2 regularization, which help prevent these issues and improve model generalization. We also explored ensemble methods like bagging, boosting, and stacking, which combine multiple models to enhance predictive accuracy.

Lastly, we touched upon the ethical and responsible use of machine learning models, emphasizing the importance of fairness, transparency, and accountability in decision-making processes. We discussed potential biases, the need for interpretability, and the importance of considering and mitigating the impact of our models on different groups.

Overall, this subchapter summarized the key concepts discussed in "Demystifying Machine Learning: A Statistical Modeling Guide for Everyone." By revisiting these concepts, we hope to have provided you with a solid foundation in statistical modeling and machine learning, enabling you to apply these techniques in a wide range of domains and niches related to statistical modeling.

Continuing Your Machine Learning Journey

Congratulations! By now, you have embarked on a remarkable journey into the world of machine learning. You have acquired a solid foundation in statistical modeling and gained insights into the fascinating field of artificial intelligence. However, your journey does not end here. In fact, it is just the beginning.

Machine learning is a rapidly evolving field, and new developments are constantly emerging. To stay ahead and continue your progress, it is essential to remain curious, committed, and adaptable. In this subchapter, we will explore various avenues for furthering your machine learning journey and expanding your knowledge in statistical modeling.

One important aspect of continuing your machine learning journey is to stay updated with the latest research and advancements. Read scientific papers, attend conferences, and join online communities to engage with experts and fellow enthusiasts. These platforms provide an excellent opportunity to gain insights, discuss ideas, and stay abreast of cutting-edge techniques and methodologies.

Practical experience is equally crucial. Apply your newfound statistical modeling skills to real-world problems and datasets. This hands-on approach will not only reinforce your understanding but also enhance your problem-solving abilities. Engage in projects, competitions, or even contribute to open-source machine learning libraries. By actively participating in these activities, you will gain invaluable experience and build a portfolio that showcases your expertise.

Additionally, consider exploring specialized areas within statistical modeling. Delve into topics like deep learning, natural language processing, or computer vision, depending on your interests. By focusing on specific niches, you can develop a deeper understanding and become proficient in applying statistical modeling techniques to solve domain-specific challenges.

Continuing your machine learning journey also involves continuous learning. Take advantage of online courses, tutorials, and resources available on platforms like Coursera, edX, or Kaggle. These platforms offer a wealth of knowledge, ranging from beginner-friendly introductions to advanced topics. Dedicate time regularly to expand your knowledge base and reinforce your understanding of statistical modeling concepts.

Lastly, embrace collaboration. Machine learning thrives on collective intelligence and collaboration. Engage in discussions, share your insights, and seek feedback from peers and mentors. Collaborative projects and discussions not only foster creativity but also expose you to different perspectives and approaches.

Remember, your machine learning journey is a lifelong endeavor. With dedication, curiosity, and continuous learning, you can unlock endless possibilities in the field of statistical modeling. Embrace the challenges, stay curious, and never cease to explore the exciting world of machine learning. Happy learning!

Final Thoughts on Demystifying Machine Learning

In this book, "Demystifying Machine Learning: A Statistical Modeling Guide for Everyone," we have explored the fascinating world of machine learning and its applications in statistical modeling. We hope that by now, you have gained a deeper understanding of this complex field and its potential to transform various industries.

Machine learning has become an essential tool for statisticians and data scientists alike. Its ability to analyze vast amounts of data, detect patterns, and make accurate predictions has revolutionized the way we approach problems in various domains. Whether you are a seasoned statistician or a curious individual looking to expand your knowledge, this book has provided you with a solid foundation to dive into the realm of machine learning.

Throughout the chapters, we have delved into different types of machine learning algorithms, from supervised learning to unsupervised learning. We have explored the concept of feature engineering, where we extract meaningful information from raw data to enhance the performance of our models. We have also discussed the importance of model evaluation and validation to ensure the reliability and generalizability of our results.

It is crucial to remember that machine learning is not a one-size-fits-all solution. Each problem requires careful consideration and selection of the appropriate algorithms and techniques. As a statistician or a data scientist, it is essential to understand the underlying assumptions and limitations of the models we build. This knowledge empowers us to make informed decisions and avoid common pitfalls.

We have also emphasized the significance of data quality and preprocessing. Machine learning models heavily rely on the input data, and any biases or errors present in the dataset can significantly impact the accuracy and fairness of our predictions. Therefore, investing time in data cleaning, handling missing values, and addressing class imbalance is vital for reliable results.

In conclusion, machine learning is a powerful tool that has the potential to revolutionize statistical modeling. It enables us to extract valuable insights from data, make accurate predictions, and drive evidence-based decision-making in various industries. However, it is crucial to approach machine learning with caution, always considering the context, limitations, and ethical implications of our models.

We hope that this book has provided you with a comprehensive understanding of machine learning and its applications in statistical modeling. Whether you are a statistician, a data scientist, or simply a curious individual, we encourage you to continue exploring this exciting field. By staying up-to-date with the latest advancements and continuously learning, you can become an expert in demystifying machine learning.